Maximised Mindpower

Maximised Mindpower

Making the Most of Your Mind

Simon Gibson

INSPIRATIONAL PRESS

Published by Inspirational Press

Copyright © 2009 Simon J Gibson

All rights reserved. This publication may not be reproduced, stored in a retrieval system or transmitted, in any form or by any means, electronic mechanical, photocopying, recording or otherwise, without the prior permission of the copyright owner.

ISBN 978-0-9562559-0-7

inspirationalpressbooks.com

"A book can change your mind..."

Contents

	About This Book	9
1	**Starters**	11
	Mindpower	12
	What does a fit mind look like?	18
	Increasing your psychological fitness	21
	Getting the most out of this book	22
	A journey of exploration	23
2	**Discover You**	27
	Pleased to meet you	28
	Getting to know you	31
	Getting to know all about you	33
3	**Attitudes**	37
	Influential predispositions	38
	Looking at our attitudes	40
	New glasses	43
4	**Life in Meaning**	47
	What's the point?	48
	What gets you up in the morning?	49
	Making a meaning matrix	50
	Deeper meaning and greater purpose	53

5	**Think Again**	59
	How good a thought manager are you?	60
	What's your thinking style?	62
	How would you like to be spoken to?	65
	What do you think?	66
	From unhelpful to helpful thinking	72
	It's how you tell the story	75
6	**Take Aim**	79
	What do you want?	80
	Keep hope alive, or hold a funeral	89
	What's your invisible problem?	91
	Don't just sit there, do something!	96
7	**Change the View**	99
	How do you feel?	100
	Anxiety and threat	106
	Anger and frustration	111
	Sadness and loss	115
	Guilt and wrong	120
	Keys to feeling good	125
8	**Body Building for the Mind**	129
	Body and mind	130
	Rest and relaxation	131
	Diet and drugs	138
	Exercise and activity	140

9	Ideas in Action	143
	What do you think you are doing?	144
	Recreation	145
	Communication	148
	Occupation	155
	Exploration	158
10	People Need People	161
	Managing relationships	162
	Find those who are good for you	163
	Forgive those who wrong you	167
	Help those you can	169
11	Strategies for Living	171
	People as strategists	172
	Check out your strategies	174
	How effective are your strategies?	180
	Changing strategies	182
12	Bouncing Back	185
	How resilient are you?	186
	Resilience training	187
13	To Infinity!	195
	Beyond yourself	196
	Meeting your deepest need	198
	Knowing what you need to know and do	201
	Overcoming your fear of death	204
	Finally	205

About This Book

This book is about making the most of your mind. The human mind is an immensely powerful generator, receiver, and transmitter of ideas. Mindpower is the name we give to this invisible force. When effectively harnessed and constructively applied, mindpower can be maximised, resulting in dramatically increased individual well being, and contributing significantly to both national and global health.

The book is designed to help you increase your mental fitness level. If I want to get physically fit, the answer is relatively simple. I can walk, run, swim, stretch, lift weights, or take up a sport, any of which will help my cause. But what if I want to increase my psychological fitness? The answer isn't quite so simple. I could practice memorisation or problem solving, but how would I know whether these exercises were enough?

The path to peak psychological fitness is both less clear and more complex than that of its physical equivalent. Because of this, people often find it hard to know how to proceed.

This book attempts to provide a clear, comprehensive and practical answer to the question of how to increase one's psychological fitness level. It does this by describing, as simply and clearly as possible, a range of strategic principles that, when understood and consistently applied, contribute significantly to enhanced psychological health and well being.

It is a book for anyone who wants to develop their mind in order to enjoy better mental health. By taking the principles described here and working with them in your own life, you will be able to increase you mental fitness level. But this book is not just for you. It is for all those whose work involves helping others to reach a place of greater mental health, personal fulfilment and psychological well being. In other words, as well as being a self-help book, it is a book for coaches, counsellors, psychotherapists, psychiatrists, and anyone whose work requires an understanding of the steps to better mental health and fitness.

My intention was to create a book that anyone could read and benefit from, rather to write solely for a more specialist academic readership. Consequently, I have sought to make the book as readable as I can by using everyday language rather than technical jargon, and by deliberately avoiding extensive references to the psychological literature that underpins many of the ideas contained in the book.

Simon Gibson 2009

1
Starters

Mindpower

Sometimes we describe people as having a brilliant mind, or as 'being' a great mind, but the truth is we have all got this amazing capability that we call mind. Though we differ from one another in many key respects, including mental abilities, even the least capable possess the marvellous phenomenon of thought.

Whatever our level of inherited ability, mind can be developed. Some people do more to develop their minds, whereas others do little or nothing in this respect, and then wonder why their lives become mediocre, or worse.

Whilst everyone has a mind capable of powerful action, not all minds are equal in capability, and not all minds have equal opportunities to develop the capability that they have. Just as people differ in height, eye colour, shoe size, and a host of other physical respects, so they differ in their mental capacities. One person may excel at playing a particular sport, another in creative activity, another in academic performance, and yet another in making friends.

The force generated by the engine of the mind is the power of thought. Like all forms of power, it may be used for good or ill; it may be used to create or destroy; it may be used responsibly or irresponsibly. In this book we are concerned with the constructive use of Mindpower.

There is, of course, a destructive use of such power, in which it is applied in the service of evil. For example, attempts at mind control are often made by those who seek to dominate, manipulate, or intimidate others for their own advantage. Such behaviour robs both individuals and nations of vitality, freedom, health, and wealth.

This book is not about making other people do what you want them to do. There are ample books of this kind already in existence. It is about taking the power of the mind, developing it, and applying it as fully as possible for your own good and for the good of your world. If it does its job properly, the book should also equip you with the skills to effectively recognise and resist those who would like to control your thinking in order to try and influence you against your will, and to make unfair gain at your expense. The title *Maximised Mindpower* reflects these aims.

Mindpower is the force of constructive thought and action, or to put it in a more technical way, it is the capacity of the mind to conceive and execute effective action in all its expressions. Mindpower is the sum of our intelligence, applied in the service of individual and group well being. It is the composite of our skill in every area of mental activity, the combined positive force of our psychological faculties, the collective beneficial impact of every psychological function.

Because of its general nature, it would be difficult, if not impossible, to come up with a single adequate test of mindpower. But it *is* perfectly possible to look at, and to some extent measure, some of the specific ways in which mindpower may be expressed.

What are these functions that together contribute to mindpower? We are looking at nothing less than the dimensions that comprise the human soul, the different modes of its operation, the various ways in which one may experience and act.

These abilities may be seen as falling into two categories: firstly, skills relating primarily to management of oneself; secondly, skills relating primarily to the management of one's immediate context. We will refer to these as personal and contextual intelligences respectively.

Personal intelligences

In the area of self management, seven distinct types of intelligence may be identified.

Intrapersonal intelligence: the degree of ability to build a good self relationship. Intrapersonal intelligence includes skill in correctly recognising our own inner experience and in managing our inner world.

Cognitive intelligence: the degree of ability to use language, to manipulate numbers, to manage sensory perceptions and mentally manipulate objects, to remember, and to engage in abstract reasoning.

Motivational intelligence: the degree of ability to find meaning in life, to choose purposes that are principled, and to live by our values, formulating successful strategies, and modifying those plans as necessary, in order to achieve specific outcomes. This includes the ability to set and to pursue achievable goals, with resilience where necessary.

Emotional intelligence: the degree of ability to effectively manage one's emotional experience. Emotional intelligence includes skill in identifying emotions, understanding their causes, resolving unhelpful emotions, generating constructive emotions, and managing emotional expression.

Bodily intelligence: the degree of ability to be aware of bodily sensations, to look after the body and to manage its needs. Bodily intelligence includes psychomotor skills such as eye-hand coordination, and kinaesthetic skill – the perception of body position, the ability to feel movements of the limbs and body, and the experience of muscular tension.

Behavioural intelligence: the degree of ability to effectively manage one's actions. Behavioural intelligence includes skill in communicating through words, tone of voice, and body language; skill in the production of artistic, literary, and musical or other creative works; skill in sports; and skill in performance arts such as music, dance, and theatre.

Spiritual intelligence: the degree of ability to effectively manage one's spiritual nature. Spiritual intelligence includes skill in drawing on the support of Infinite Intelligence in order to transcend the limitations of our finite human nature.

Contextual intelligences

In the area of self context management, two further broad types of intelligence may be observed.

Interpersonal intelligence: the degree of ability to relate well to others. Interpersonal intelligence includes skill in correctly interpreting other people's words, tone of voice, and body language.

Material intelligence: the degree of ability to manage the non-human aspects of one's personal context. Material intelligence involves skill in relating to non-human structures and systems, such as managing personal finances, car maintenance, and gardening.

As we look at human abilities in this way, it is important to recognise that these are broad categories, far from watertight, with significant overlap between them. Many tasks draw on a number of these intelligences simultaneously. For example, I have cited gardening as an example of material intelligence, because it involves interaction with the non-human context, but gardening draws on other intelligences also, including cognitive intelligence (it requires thought), bodily intelligence (you need to know where your limbs are), and behavioural intelligence (specific actions are involved).

Taken together, these categories represent a set of interrelated mental abilities or intelligences. The interrelationship is a complex one, especially as each of these areas is made up of even more specific intelligences. For example, management of our inner world, a characteristic of intrapersonal intelligence, involves linking thoughts, feelings and actions in combinations that are meaningful to us. Attitudinal intelligence is the ability to do this well, so that we develop and maintain constructive perspectives on things, learning to think, feel and behave towards people (or objects) in helpful ways.

All these intelligences draw on inherited potential, but are developed through training. With appropriate education each individual may attain their highest level of intelligence in each mode. This book is written to help you develop selected skills in each of these intelligences: the skills that contribute most, in the author's opinion, to high levels of psychological well being and mental health.

Because our focus is on building psychological health, we will not be explaining how to develop all the skills represented by each type of intelligence. Apart from being a task of vast proportions, requiring many volumes, it is unnecessary for our purpose, which is to selectively focus on those particular abilities that contribute most significantly to high levels of mental fitness. Whilst it might be argued that developing any psychological skill may add something to our overall well being, some skills are central to greater psychological health, and it is these that we'll be working on.

What are these skills? Or, to put the question another way, ...

What does a fit mind look like?

What are the characteristics of the psychologically fit? People with high levels of psychological fitness are better at managing both their inner world of experience, and their outer world of behaviour and relationships. Compared with their less mentally fit counterparts, they deal more effectively with the changes and challenges of life, they manage the resulting stress better, and they are better able to bounce back when bad things happen.

More specifically, fit minds display characteristics such as the following:

- An effective strategy for living
- A good self relationship
- A constructive set of core attitudes that promote self realisation
- A sense of meaning and purpose in life
- An ability to recognise and change unhelpful or inaccurate thoughts
- An ability to set and to pursue achievable goals
- Good emotional self management
- Adequate care of the body and management of its needs
- Constructive behaviour patterns
- An ability to relate well to others
- Resilience in dealing with the environment, its opportunities and demands
- A transcendent perspective on life

These positive features are the invisible inner ingredients that make for quality of life. They enable us to experience life most richly, manage it most effectively, and live it most fully. They are the characteristics of those who engage with life, and who make a difference, not merely through productive activity and meaningful relationships, but by that phenomenon of psychological osmosis whereby humans are influenced by leaders, whether for good or ill. They are the fitness factors for maximised mindpower that we will be seeking to build through the pages of this book.

Whilst we are looking at the characteristics of a fit mind, it is probably a good idea for us to also consider what psychological health is not. This is a helpful exercise because people often have inaccurate ideas about this area. Here are some of the myths and misconceptions that I have come across concerning mental health:

- Psychologically healthy people never get upset about anything
- Psychologically healthy people always think logically
- Psychologically healthy people consistently talk with calm rationality
- Psychologically healthy people never do anything strange or unusual
- Psychologically healthy people are consistently unemotional

Let us debunk these erroneous ideas:

- Psychological health is **not** completely avoiding getting upset – mentally healthy people get upset about things, but they manage their upsets in constructive ways
- Psychological health is **not** restricting your thinking to logic alone – people with fit minds engage in various kinds of thinking that include intuition, creativity, aesthetic appreciation, and observation, to name only a few

- Psychological health is **not** being calmly intellectual at all times – a fit mind can express itself in a range of ways appropriate to the person's character
- Psychological health is **not** the absence of strange or unusual behaviour – those who enjoy a high level of psychological health are not slavishly conformist, but are able to express their own uniqueness and individuality in ways that are appropriate but which may sometimes appear odd to others
- Psychological health is **not** remaining coolly unemotional – emotionally healthy people face their feelings, express them appropriately, and mange them effectively

Increasing your psychological fitness

Just as some physically healthy people are fitter than others, so those who are mentally healthy differ in terms of their mental fitness level. In the same way that physical fitness may be increased through physical exercise, good diet, and other disciplines, so mental fitness can be enhanced by exercising the mind, controlling what we put into it, and developing its power for good.

When it comes to their psychological health, it is not unusual for people to wait until something goes wrong before they take action. Many assume that they are mentally healthy, and do not realise that they could be even fitter, enjoying greater self-mastery and fulfilment. It is only when they experience some kind of 'breakdown' that such people go for help to 'fix' the problem. Ironically, a psychological crisis of this kind might never have arisen, had the person realised the value of developing their mind and of keeping mentally fit through regular psychological exercise.

By disciplined practice, not only can you make more of your mind, you can make the most of your mind.

Getting the most out of this book

To get the most out of this book, I suggest that you do three things. Firstly, read with a hunger to know the truth, even where that truth is challenging, painful, or contrary to what you have believed up to now, and when you find it, be willing to change your mind where necessary. Secondly, take the steps indicated in each chapter, completing each exercise. Thirdly, practice these principles daily until they become an automatic part of your everyday life.

A journey of exploration

If you are going to take a journey, or take others on a journey, it makes sense to get hold of an accurate map. This is no less true concerning the journey of personal development towards maximised mindpower, than it is for any physical expedition. Although an abstraction from the reality it represents, a good map may help you find your way, so that you are better equipped to explore that reality, and to arrive at your desired destination.

When it comes to a map of human psychology, we face serious challenges posed by the complexity of individuals and the great variations between them. Making a half decent map of one person is a significant project, before we start trying to build a map that will be applicable to all. Thankfully, humans do have generic characteristics, so it is possible to produce general guidelines and frameworks that are relevant and helpful to everyone. This book contains just such a framework. But deciding on just what those shared characteristics are is easier said than done.

Early in my work as a psychologist, I began to find that so much of what I identified in people could not be explained by existing theories. So instead of trying to explain what I saw using available frameworks and maps, I began to simply observe, allowing a picture to gradually form.

I realised that, having taken this path, I was looking at emerging themes. Slowly, like the opening of a flower, patterns of meaning would unfold, sometimes telling a very different story to that of current theory. Increasingly, I became convinced that the analysis of these life themes was central to a proper understanding of human experience and behaviour. Life Theme

Analysis (LTA) was the result: a new psychological theory, and a practical tool for promoting individual and group well being.

LTA is concerned with the uniqueness of the individual and works with that uniqueness. Like planets, people have shared characteristics, but knowledge of these general characteristics can only tell us so much. Knowing that a planet is a spherical body and that it orbits the sun might be helpful facts, but they tell us nothing about the terrain of that world. We need to go beyond knowledge of shared characteristics, and find out what that particular planet is actually like.

LTA seeks to do this in relation to human psychology. Although, like all models, it provides a general framework for understanding, LTA is more a way of map making than a map for making a way. Everyone is different. Therefore each must be represented by their own unique and continuously developing map. By working with themes, and only by working with themes, it is possible to develop that personal picture.

The challenge we face, whether we are pursuing our own personal development, or working with others to promote theirs, is to become map makers. We need to train people in map making, rather than just give them more maps. A general theory can never adequately describe an individual.

In LTA, life themes are understood to be meaningful patterns of experience and behaviour. Whilst many themes may be shared by individuals, no two people will ever have an identical set of themes.

This book sets out, not just to give you the general principles you need to know, but to help you explore your own unique set of themes relating to psychological well being, and then work with those themes to maximise your mindpower.

I would like to encourage you to think of yourself as an explorer. Just as an explorer of old would set out on a voyage of discovery into the unknown, with the hope of charting foreign shores, so you are embarking on an inner journey, no less challenging, but one from which you may return with knowledge of inner places you never visited before, and with that knowledge gain mastery of the world within.

2
Discover You

Pleased to meet you

I find it ironic, that of all human relationships, the closest and most intimate union of all is frequently unrecognised and even more frequently undeveloped: the self relationship.

Self relationship is simply the relationship you have with yourself. Humans have the ability to reflect on themselves, which means that they have attitudes, thoughts and feelings about themselves, just as they have attitudes, thoughts and feelings about other people, and many other things too for that matter.

Everyone has a self relationship, but not everyone has a good self relationship. For many, a poor self relationship is simply the legacy of not having done any work in this foundational area of personal development. Their view of themselves and their attitudes towards themselves have grown in a piecemeal fashion over the course of their life to date, and the resulting composite image has never been properly evaluated to check either its accuracy or value.

Amongst this group are those whose poor self relationship is driven by the fact that they have taken a dislike to themselves. If you don't like you, then you probably won't get along too well with yourself. This can lead to all kinds of problems, and rob you of psychological health.

Whatever the causes, a poor self relationship leads to problems, one way or another. If you are divided against yourself internally, the conflict within will rob you of both time and energy. Unresolved, it will claim your attention and drain your resources, so that you are unable to live your life to the full.

A good self relationship is just what it says: being your own friend. If I were to ask you whether you were living in harmonious relationship with yourself, what would your answer be? If you consistently relate to yourself in a negative, unfriendly, or deceitful way, you have a poor self-relationship.

A simple technique for assessing self relationship is to listen to your inner dialogue. Talking to yourself inside your own head is perfectly normal. The things we say to ourselves in the privacy of our own minds can tell us a great deal about the nature of the self relationship.

Talk to yourself for a minute or two (not out loud, unless you are on your own and cannot be overheard – people may think you're crazy if they hear you talking to yourself in public!) What do you hear?

Now appraise what you just heard. Here are some questions to help you:

- How would you describe your manner towards yourself? What adjectives would you use? (E.g. friendly, unfriendly, patronising, helpful, dismissive, rude, or ...?)
- Is this how you usually relate to yourself?
- Based on what you hear, how would you describe your general attitude towards yourself?
- Are there other specific attitudes that you can identify from your self-talk? If so, what are they?
- Do you regularly encourage yourself or run yourself down?
- Does your inner dialogue tend to be positive or negative?
- If someone else spoke to you in the way you generally speak to yourself, how would you feel and what would be your response?

Honestly answered, questions like these can help us build a picture of how we treat ourselves. How does that picture look for you? Stop for a moment and create a sentence that describes your present self relationship.

Now consider the implications of such a relationship for your day to day experience. To make it easier, I suggest that you think of the implications in relation to some specific areas. For example, how might your present self relationship influence:

- What you think?
- How you feel?
- The way you act?
- Your happiness?
- Your relationships with others?
- Your achievements?
- Your career?

You may find it helpful to write a few sentences describing the implications as you see them. Thinking of possible implications can be a good way of evaluating your present self relationship.

It may be that as you look at how you currently relate to yourself, you recognise that your present self relationship might benefit from some constructive development work.

Building a good self-relationship requires a decision to be friendly and stay friendly towards you. If you have not already done so, you can make that decision right now.

Getting to know you

Before you can take the step of becoming your own friend, you may need to do some work on what you see when you look at yourself. The reason for this is simple. The way you see yourself (self concept) and your evaluation of yourself (self esteem), both influence the way you relate to yourself. For example, if you see yourself as unintelligent (self concept), and you despise your low intelligence (self esteem), you may find it easier to become your own enemy than your own friend!

Some people are in the position of being their own worst enemy. Because they dislike one or more of their perceived characteristics, they develop an attitude of opposition towards themselves.

Whilst a healthy dislike of specific attitudes or traits may be wholly appropriate, and contribute powerfully to personal development, the development of a negatively biased general evaluation of oneself frequently leads to problems. Low self esteem can undermine your confidence, increase your stress levels, and lead to defensive or compensatory behaviour. It has been linked to various conditions, including mood disorders, drug and alcohol abuse, chronic fatigue, and eating disorders.

What's the answer? Sometimes we may need to change our self concept. If we have developed an inaccurate view of ourselves, that view needs to change. For example, someone who was repeatedly called stupid as a child and who came to believe it was true, despite being of average intelligence or above, now needs to change their view to a more accurate one. It is likely that the new view will make them more attractive in their own eyes, and then they'll find it easier to be their own friend.

By developing a more accurate self concept, we may find ourselves more likeable. But there is a problem: we cannot guarantee this outcome. An accurate view of oneself does not necessarily mean that we will find ourselves more attractive. In fact, it may have the opposite effect! We may not like what we see.

Looking at ourselves honestly and accurately is an important part of building a good self relationship. When we know someone well, we are better able to work with them. This is as true of the self relationship as it is of any other. But a good self relationship depends as much on the attitudes we hold towards ourselves, as it does on the information we know about ourselves.

Whatever the facts about us, we face the challenge of adopting a friendly stance in relation to ourselves. As far as our characteristics are concerned, there will be things we like and things we do not like, things we approve of and things we do not approve of. We need a love for ourselves that neither denigrates the good, nor sanitises the bad.

If you have got a healthy self friendship you will want to get to know yourself as fully as possible, and you will be willing to face both positive and negative aspects. Also, you will love yourself despite your unacceptable side. The unacceptable remains unacceptable. You retain the capacity to be upset by such characteristics, and you work to change them for the better wherever possible. In contrast, unhealthy self love tends to ignore or deny less desirable characteristics, and to exaggerate or even fabricate positive traits and actions.

The first step towards a good self relationship takes but a moment. This is the decision to be your own friend that you value. If you have never made that decision, or if you made it previously but have let it slip, why not make it now.

Getting to know all about you

The second step takes a little longer. This is the day by day building of an excellent relationship with yourself as you really are. As you develop such a relationship, you will find that it has the potential to contribute powerfully towards your self-confidence and self-esteem.

The name we give to this developmental path is self realisation. Self realisation is the process of becoming yourself and realising your individual capacity for constructive experience and action.

Self realisation is *not* becoming everything that one is capable of becoming. The choice of one developmental path inevitably means the rejection of another. You may have the potential to become a world-class concert pianist, a good cook, a ground-breaking neurosurgeon, an amateur boat builder, a tiddlywinks champion, a Nobel Prize winner, a three chord guitarist, a great statesperson, and countless other things, but you do not have time to become them all!

Full realisation of one's potential in this life is an existential impossibility. Self realisation *does* involve the realisation of one's potential, but only as far as possible, given the various limitations of personal resources and context.

How do we get to know our true selves well and build a good self relationship? The decision to be your own friend is vital, but it needs to be accompanied by self awareness if the relationship is going to be a healthy one.

Self awareness is the fruit of self examination. By looking honestly at yourself, from a place of friendship, you may come to know yourself increasingly well. But what exactly are you looking at?

If you don't know what to look for, you might miss important information. All of us need a basic knowledge of the different dimensions that make up a human being. Without such knowledge you may fail to see key aspects of yourself, and such ignorance may prove costly to your well being. Imagine how the safety of a car would be compromised if the mechanic working on it had no knowledge of brakes.

Let's take a brief look at some of the dimensions that may be said to characterise every human person. As we are focusing on the significance of the self relationship, the concept of the self might be a good place to start.

The term 'self' can be used to refer either to what you see when you look at yourself or to the 'you' that does the seeing. The first is the self as perceived, experienced, and known, whilst the second is the self that perceives, experiences, and knows, the 'you' that is reading this sentence right now.

When you look at yourself, there are a number of aspects that may be directly observed. The information available to you includes ideas about the present and memories from the past (cognition); choices you could make, and things you could aim for (motivation); information on how you feel (emotion); data from your senses (perception), 'gut feelings' you have about certain things (intuition); and action choices available to you (behaviour).

As the manager of all these personal resources, you decide what you are going to attend to, when you are going to attend to it, how much attention you are going to give it, how you are going to view it, what decisions you are going to make (if any) in response to it, and how you are going to act (or not) in the light of it. You are the one who decides which information to consider and which information to reject. You are the one who decides on what action to take. In short, you're in charge!

But what are you like as a boss? How good are you at running the operation that is your own life? By adopting a healthy attitude of friendship towards yourself, you are much more likely to manage your inner and outer life in a constructive way, but you will still need to work on it. The way you have learnt to run your life may contain bad habits that now need to be identified and changed if you are going to enjoy the best self relationship possible.

Each chapter of this book addresses a different aspect of you, and is constructed to help you discover this part of yourself and to increase your level of self mastery in it. You can only make the most of your mind if you manage it well.

3
Attitudes

Influential predispositions

As creators or destroyers of opportunity, attitudes exert a profound influence on our psychological well being. Good attitudes can increase our psychological fitness, open doors of opportunity, and move us forwards into new places of growth and fulfilment. Bad attitudes, on the other hand, can undermine our well being, close doors of opportunity, and push us backwards into states of dysfunction and self induced disappointment.

Think of a person who goes to work with a willing and helpful attitude that contributes to a healthy self-esteem, results in their becoming valued, and leads to their being given opportunities such as further training or promotion. Contrast this with someone who approaches their work with a grudging and resentful attitude that poisons their outlook on life, results in their becoming avoided by others, and leads to their being sidelined and passed over when it comes to employment opportunities.

What is an attitude? A classic definition that has generally enjoyed wide acceptance by psychologists over many years is that of Gordon Allport who defined attitude as, "A learned predisposition to think, feel and behave toward a person (or object) in a particular way."

Attitudes are the internal positions we adopt in relation to objects of every kind. They prepare people for action, are learned from experience, and exert a motivating force on behaviour. In short, they profoundly influence the way in which we respond. We begin to appreciate the vast extent of this influence when we recognise that everything conceived in a human mind may have an attitude, or attitudes, associated with it.

To a large extent we choose our attitudes. Each is a position you take in relation to yourself, other objects, or groups of objects, predisposing you to respond to them in certain ways. Every type of response is affected, including thoughts, feelings and actions. Once adopted, an attitude will consistently influence the way you see its object.

Like a pair of glasses that adjust your vision, enabling you to see close up, far off, or in bright sunlight, your attitudes change the way you see things. Whatever you look at through those attitudinal glasses is influenced accordingly. For example, seen through the glasses of confidence life seems manageable; seen through the glasses of fear life appears threatening; seen through the glasses of despair life looks hopeless.

As these examples show, attitudes may be helpful or unhelpful, representing positive or negative viewpoints and enlightened or unenlightened perspectives. Negative, unenlightened, or otherwise unhelpful attitudes, may predispose you to inaccurate or dysfunctional thinking, unpleasant or inappropriate emotions, and potentially damaging behaviour.

Given these toxic effects, it is not hard to see how bad attitudes may be responsible for a great deal of human suffering and lack. Whatever your unhelpful attitudes may be, they represent a constant threat, not only to your own well being, but also to that of those around you. Such attitudes need to give way to helpful and positive ones if you are going to enjoy greater mental fitness. When we change our attitudes for the better, we benefit both ourselves and others. Each one of us faces the challenge of developing and maintaining a helpful, positive and enlightened outlook that will help us to move towards life rather than run from it.

Looking at our attitudes

Because attitudes have a focus, we cannot say that we understand any attitude unless we have identified the object, or category of objects, to which it relates. The object of an attitude may be concrete (e.g. this book) or abstract (e.g. the theory contained within it), animate (e.g. your pet) or inanimate (e.g. a pet shop), individual (e.g. your next door neighbour) or group (e.g. other people in general).

Saying that someone has a resentful attitude only tells us so much about them. We cannot predict when and where they will act resentfully unless we know who or what the attitude is aimed at. Without this knowledge, we do not know whether they will be resentful towards other people in general, or towards those whom they see as better off than themselves, or towards those they work with, or towards some other individual or group.

Attitudes are generally a good guide to behaviour, but it is important to be aware that there is no guarantee that a person will always act in accordance with them. There are situations where people may behave contrary to their stated attitudes. For example, someone acting under extreme stress might act out of character. However, despite this, it remains the case that people are more likely to act in accordance with the attitudes they hold, than in other ways.

When we start looking at attitudes, we are soon struck by their sheer number. Each human mind contains a great many attitudes. This is hardly surprising, given that every person, item, or event in our experience has attitudes related to it.

Whilst all attitudes exert an influence on the way we experience and act, some are more influential than others. For example, a rejecting attitude towards a particular TV programme is likely to cause you fewer problems than an arrogant attitude towards other people.

Attitudes often go undetected. In fact, in view of the very large number of attitudes held by each individual, it is inevitable that many will remain hidden. If we have held a particular attitude for some time, we may get to a place where it becomes not only an automatic response, but also an unconscious one. Obviously, this is not a problem if the unseen attitude is healthy, but failure to recognise our unhealthy attitudes may mean that we continue to be robbed of things we value, without ever identifying the toxic agents behind them.

Given that unrecognised bad attitudes may be responsible for some of the pain and disappointment that we have experienced it makes sense to look at our attitudes and to change them wherever necessary. We face the challenge of ensuring, as far as possible, that our attitudes are constructive ones that enhance our experience and enjoyment of life.

So let's take a look at some of our attitudes. As it would probably take many books to deal adequately with the vast number of different attitudes that may be held, not to mention the relation of those attitudes to psychological well being, we are going to limit our focus to some of the general attitudes that influence a wide range of our responses. The larger the category of objects to which an attitude relates, the more influential that attitude is likely to be, in terms of the scope of its influence.

Attitudes to life, other people in general, and work, are good examples here. As a simple exercise for exploring your own attitudes, I invite you to complete the following sentences. Give the answer that first comes to mind.

- Life is …
- People are …
- Work is …

By responding with the first words that come into your head, you are more likely to capture attitudes that you may not be fully conscious of, or perhaps attitudes you disapprove of in yourself, but which reflect how you feel at this particular moment.

Now repeat the exercise, but this time think carefully about the way you complete each sentence. Your answers may be different this time, as they are more likely to express attitudes reflecting your considered views, principles and values.

You can use this technique to explore attitudes to anything. Just substitute its name, and create a sentence. What you come up with will tell you something about your attitude to that thing. Whatever the object, asking the question, "Where do I stand in relation to this?" will help you to build a clearer and fuller understanding of your own attitudes to it.

Identifying our attitudes is the first step towards developing them. The next step is evaluation. Whenever we recognise one of our own attitudes, we should take a moment to evaluate its influence in our life. The more honest we are about the nature and impact of our attitudes, the better informed we will be when we come to build new and better ones.

At the heart of evaluation is the question of whether the attitude adds to our mental fitness and mindpower, or undermines it. We need to know whether the attitude is a true expression of who we are, and whether it makes us think better thoughts and do better things.

We have seen that self realisation is the process of becoming ourselves and realising our individual capacity for constructive experience and action. The attitudes we hold may promote that process, retard it, or even put it into reverse. So a good question to ask of any attitude is whether it increases the well being of both the individual and of humanity in general.

New glasses

Because they are learnt predispositions, attitudes *can* be changed. Existing unhelpful attitudes may be replaced by new helpful ones. This involves adopting a new position and practising it until it becomes automatic. By monitoring our own attitudes and consistently modifying them for the better in this way, it becomes possible to develop constructive attitudes in every area of life. As we do, our inner experience changes, as thoughts, feelings, and intended actions increasingly reflect the new positions we have chosen.

Some attitudes are unhelpful because of their negative polarity. Many people struggle with negative attitudes and their effects. You may like to try the following exercise as a way of strengthening your own positive outlook. Place a notebook and pen by your bed and at the end of each day write down three or four good things that happened to you during the day. Keep it up for a week and you may be struck by how much more positive you feel. What you are doing in this exercise is re-training yourself to focus on the good rather than on the bad. Given the fact that the untrained mind seems to revert to negative thinking, you may want to continue the exercise after the week is over, in order to help ensure that your positive outlook remains in place.

A common negative attitude that undermines peoples' mental fitness and fulfilment is the predisposition to see oneself primarily as a victim. The truth is that we are all victims in some way. Everyone experiences to some degree the consequences of human injustice, greed, and folly, whether directly or indirectly. It's not the recognition of this fact that causes people problems, but an exaggerated emphasis upon it.

The person with a victim attitude tends to see only the various ways in which they have been cheated, robbed, let down, or treated unfairly and unjustly. Such a bias tends to lead inevitably to feeling sorry for oneself much of the time, holding pity parties in which one complains to oneself and anyone else who'll listen (or even those who won't), and an expectation that the future will be no different than the past. This mentality easily traps its owners in a prison of negativity and helplessness from which they may be unable to recognise or respond to current opportunities.

If you feel that you have fallen into the trap of seeing yourself as a victim, you may find it helpful to write a new description of yourself that portrays you more as an agent of positive influence and change, than as a victim of negative events and experiences. Then read and practice this every day until it becomes your accustomed view and habitual manner.

Another common characteristic of unhelpful attitudes is that they are inadequately informed by the truth. The way we see things may reflect ignorance, denial, or distortion of the facts. Often, people just don't see what's happening, so their views are based on inaccurate information, and this can lead to problems. When they do see what's going on, they may not like what they see. At such a moment they are faced with a choice: face the facts you find threatening, reject them, or construct an alternative reality.

Be careful when you make assumptions about yourself, other people, and things. Remember that these may or may not be correct. Check them out, as far as you can, to establish their validity. Take the time to find out the truth, as far as you can. You may be glad you did later.

If someone sees a source of information as authoritative they are more likely to believe what it says. This is why people often uncritically accept what they read in books, or even in magazines and newspapers. They assume that because it's in print, it is true – a dangerous assumption. Similarly, people often unquestioningly believe the pronouncements of those they trust or respect, again a potentially dangerous mistake. However authoritative the source may appear to be, check it out!

Much avoidable bias and many prejudiced attitudes arise from conclusions made on the basis of inadequate or incorrect data. Try to get your facts right before you adopt an attitude, and be ready to adjust your attitude where necessary as you get new information and insights. A radical commitment to truth (itself an attitude) will help you stay on track here.

Now let's return to the sentences you completed earlier. What do your statements say about your attitudes? Against each statement, write down the attitude, or attitudes, it seems to express.

Next, take the attitudes that you have identified, and evaluate them one by one. In your view, is each one helpful or unhelpful, positive or negative, well informed or uninformed, a constructive response to the things you fear or an inappropriately avoidant one?

For each attitude that you feel needs working on, decide on what you need to do to correct it, or to make it even better than it is. What action is required? If you need to get more information, do so. Find the available facts. If you need to take a more positive slant, do so. Be honest, but accentuate the positive. If you recognise a biased or prejudiced viewpoint that you need to correct, do so. Get your objectivity back.

Don't limit your work to the attitudes that you feel need some attention. Remember that good attitudes can often be made even better. Take a look at attitudes you think are OK, and ask yourself how they might be developed further.

A helpful next step is to write a brief statement describing your new viewpoint. This is the position you now choose to adopt in relation to that thing. What does your new view look like? Write a brief statement describing it. It need only be a few sentences or a paragraph at most. On completing this exercise, you will have a description of your new attitude. All that remains now is to implement that attitude.

Implementation is all about practice. Read the statement of your new attitude at the start of every day and at any other time you feel the need to remind yourself of where you now stand. Each time you affirm your new view and put it into practice, it will get stronger. In a few weeks time, you will reach a point where you have learnt the new attitude and no longer need to refer to your written statement. It will have become an automatic response and a natural part of your everyday life.

4
Life in Meaning

What's the point?

Minds appear to work best when enriched by meaning and moved by purpose.

Both meaning and purpose relate to what we value and consider important. The difference between the two concepts reflects a fundamental psychological distinction between experience and behaviour. When we find things meaningful, it is because we experience them as valuable, they matter to us. If meaning is more a state of being, then purpose is more a state of doing, an experience of actual or intended action. When our actions are purposeful, it is because we are doing what matters to us, the things we value.

Meaning and purpose are like twins, in that they often appear together. We tend to pursue the things we find meaningful, and we tend to attach meaning to the things we pursue.

From early in life, each of us makes decisions about what we value. We attach meaning to things. Although surrounded by messages telling us what we should value, we decide on what is meaningful to us, and what purposes are worthwhile. Despite the often powerful influence of social and cultural values, ultimately it is a personal choice.

People find meaning in different things. I recall once hearing about a sufferer from anorexia who became so interested in stained glass windows that she lost interest in losing weight and instead became engrossed in the study of stained glass.

Meaning is important. People find it harder to do things that lack meaning for them. They find it much easier to do things, if they understand the purpose of the task, the point of the activity. If there is no purpose to your life, why live?

What gets you up in the morning?

What are the things that matter to you? What's important to you? What gets you up in the morning (apart from the alarm)? Questions like these are helpful because they get us looking at our own experience of meaning and purpose, and the way in which that experience adds to (or detracts from) our psychological well being.

I am going to invite you to look at your life and identify those areas that particularly give your life meaning. Here are some questions to help you. I suggest that you write down your answers to each one. As you do, be honest, write what first comes to you, and try not to censor your responses.

- What gives your life meaning?
- What are the things that matter most to you in life?
- What kinds of things get you out of bed in the morning?
- What do you live for?
- What is it about your life that makes a positive difference in the lives of others?
- What does a good day look like for you? If you were to review the day, before you sleep, what characteristics would make it a success?
- What would you like other people to say about you when you're dead?

You may find that there is a lot of overlap between your responses to each of these questions. That's fine. The point of the questions is to help you explore this area and build a picture of the principal things that give your life meaning and purpose.

Now take your written answers, identify the sources of meaning and purpose that they contain, and write a list of these.

Making a meaning matrix

Next, count up the items on your list, take a blank piece of paper, and divide it up so that you have got the same number of areas as items. Write the names of the items in the areas, one in each. When you have finished, you will have what I call a meaning matrix. Here is an example:

Partner	Work	Creativity
Family	Faith	Sport

    A device of this kind shows you, at a glance, the principal areas of meaning that you are currently aware of in your life. Should you become aware of further areas, you can restructure the matrix at any time to accommodate new categories.
    What does your matrix tell you? I suggest you look at two things in particular. Firstly, the total number of categories

represented, and secondly, what each of those categories means to you.

We will start by looking at the total number of categories. A grid with many sections may suggest a life seen as rich in meaning and purpose, whereas a grid with few sections may suggest the opposite. However, we should be careful to bear in mind that the latter does not necessarily reflect a lack of passion or intensity of purpose. The number of categories itself tells us nothing about strength of purpose.

Having a larger number of meaningful areas in your life, may mean that you cope better with loss than those who have fewer areas of meaning. Imagine someone who has only one such area: their job. Should they lose that job, the loss is likely to be particularly devastating, as their work represented their sole source of meaning and purpose. In contrast, the person with two areas in their matrix is in a stronger position, for if they lose one source of meaning they still have the other. Those with a broader spread of meaningful areas are in an even better position. Generally speaking, it might be said that the more objects of meaning we enjoy, the stronger we will be in the face of loss. We will still experience grief, perhaps intensely, but we have not lost everything that we live for. There are still resources of meaning and purpose that remain.

If, when you completed the above exercise, you could not identify any areas of meaning or sense of purpose, it may be because you have recently been bereaved, or it may indicate that you are suffering from depression. If you have not recently experienced a major loss, and you are experiencing a pervasive sense of meaninglessness or hopelessness, you should see a physician to check for depression, and, if necessary, receive treatment. You should do this, even if you have identified one or more areas of meaning, but are also experiencing an ongoing low mood or sense of hopelessness.

A second way in which we can learn from our meaning matrix is to look more closely at what each of the categories represents for us. You can do this by taking each item on your grid, and writing a one or two sentence paragraph on the subject of 'What This Means to Me'.

Having completed this exercise, you may find that you are more aware than before of the relative value you ascribe to each area of meaning. Although all the categories are meaningful for you, some will probably be more meaningful than others.

With this in mind, rank the categories on your grid in order of their value to you. Give what you value most the rank of 1, the second most valuable area a 2, and so on, until you have ranked them all.

If you have identified and ranked your areas of meaning and purpose correctly, the item you have ranked first will represent your primary area of meaning. Because they matter most to us, high ranking areas are powerful motivators whose influence pervades our whole life.

The depressed person disillusioned by broken dreams, the busy person filling their emptiness with activity, and the dying person regretting how they have spent their life, may all be suffering from the consequences of failing to find and follow an adequate primary source of meaning and purpose.

Deeper meaning and greater purpose

If an experience of deeper meaning and greater purpose will help us make the most of our mind and increase our psychological well being, how do we achieve it?

We have already taken the first step, by exploring our own areas of meaning and purpose. Equipped with that understanding, we now need to look at how these areas might be developed. Here are some suggestions you might like to consider.

Adding new areas of meaning

However many compartments there may be in your meaning matrix, you can always increase the number of areas represented. By expanding the range of areas that you find particularly meaningful, you may increase your overall sense of meaning and purpose. Why not choose a new interest today?

Adding new areas of meaning is particularly important if you can only identify a few areas. We have already reflected on the potential dangers of this position. If you have just one or two areas of meaning on your grid, look for additional areas to add. You can add new areas of meaning to your life at any time.

Increasing our appreciation of existing areas of meaning

The fact that we find certain things especially meaningful does not necessarily mean that we will get the full psychological benefit from what we value. If I own a beautiful painting but never look at it, I deprive myself of much pleasure that was potentially mine. Often, it is only when we start to meditate or reflect on the thing valued that we start to experience a deeper appreciation for it.

That is why it is good to stop every now and then, and express your appreciation for the things you love, the things you value, the things that give your life meaning and purpose.

If you want to go into a little more depth on this, take your meaning matrix and spend five or ten minutes reflecting on the value of each area, writing down as many ways you can think of in which this area enriches and benefits your life. This may help you to expand your appreciation of the area concerned.

Ensuring that our purposes are principled

Another way of raising the impact that meaning and purpose can have on our peace and well being, is to evaluate each area on our grid in terms of our principles and core values. If we're investing meaning in areas contrary to our moral and ethical values, or pursuing what we feel are legitimate purposes but in a way that contravenes our deeply held principles, the outcome will be inner dissonance and tension rather than enhanced well being and peace of mind.

The answer is to bring the contents of our meaning matrix, and the actions associated with them, into agreement with our moral values. The resulting congruence will help to ensure that the benefits to our well being are optimised. Not all purpose is equally beneficial to psychological health and mindpower. A principled purpose that is congruent with our moral values will have the most beneficial effect.

Changing our primary sources of meaning

Primary objects of meaning can be replaced by others. People may change their primary sources of meaning as a result of dissatisfaction with existing sources, attraction to new sources, or a mixture of the two.

Sometimes people reach a place where they feel that the sources of meaning that have given their life purpose, perhaps for many years, are inadequate in some way. Growing disillusionment with existing sources may mean that a person is increasingly unhappy and open to change. This often precedes the adoption of a new primary purpose.

Experiences of disillusionment are potentially enlightening. The appearance of disillusionment may suggest that we were under an illusion in the first place. Disillusion can drive us to look at alternative sources of meaning and purpose that are better than the ones we have lost. But disillusion without a new source of meaning can be a dark path, often characterised by unhappiness, boredom, or depression.

In contrast to change driven by dissatisfaction, changes to primary sources of meaning may be brought about by the discovery of what is seen as a new and greater purpose. The recognition of a new source of meaning that is perceived to be better than existing sources, usually results in this object becoming the new primary area of meaning.

Adding meaning and purpose to work

When people lack meaning in work, it affects both their contentment and their contribution. Because work is a major component of most people's lives, it is helpful to a person's psychological well being if it is experienced as meaningful.

How valuable is your work to you? To what degree is it a meaningful part of your life? To make the most of your mind, you need to find some meaning in what you do. If you cannot find meaning in what you do, you will probably struggle to do it.

You have various options when it comes to increasing the meaningfulness of your work. One is to change your job for another that is more meaningful to you. It may or may not be possible to change the paid work that you do. If it isn't, you need to look at options two and three.

A second option is to make changes to the nature of your present job, the way that you do the job, or the way that you see the job, so that it becomes more meaningful. The challenge of finding meaning in work that you do not enjoy, or for which your temperament is unsuited, can be very great indeed, but it is not impossible.

A third option is to start doing some work of your own choice, something you believe in, as a second job, or as your only occupation if you are not currently in paid employment. Irrespective of whether you are paid for this work, the fact that it is meaningful to you will itself be rich payment. What kind of work could you do that you would value? Start doing it, or something as close to it as you can get, and you will add meaning to your work.

Living by what we value

It's one thing to find meaning and purpose, but another to live by it. Every day we face a fundamental choice. We can choose to follow what is most important to us, or we can compromise our values.

Sometimes people put off doing the things they believe in until later. In a world full of pressures and demands, it is easy to sacrifice the important for the urgent. A person may try to clear the urgent tasks before doing what is important to them, only to find that further urgent matters now clamour for their attention!

There are two main problems with this approach. Firstly, valuable time and other resources are wasted that could have been spent in the service of one's highest purpose. Secondly, the person may run out of time, never arriving at that place where they do what matters most to them. Don't wait until you have dealt with urgent matters. Start doing what is important to you now. Start today.

Make each day count by doing what you believe is most important. Live by what you value.

5
Think Again

How good a thought manager are you?

Thoughts hurt or heal. Every thought you have ever had, every thought you are having now, and every thought you will ever have, is related in some way to your psychological fitness. Your experience, your actions, and the way your life unfolds, are all influenced by what and how you think. Truly, thoughts are powerful things. Choose your conscious thoughts carefully, for each one will help to shape your destiny.

Just as certain forms of thinking promote psychological well being, other kinds of thinking are related to mental health problems. When we change the way we think our mood changes, and we move either towards greater peace of mind or towards deeper dysfunction.

Thoughts come in many different colours, shapes, and sizes. For example, we have ideas, we form opinions, we visualise, we reflect, we reason, we remember, we plan, and we try to solve problems. The ability to do these things we call cognitive intelligence.

Managing thoughts of every kind is a challenge we all face. There is hardly a moment of our waking life when we are not choosing what to think about, or how to think about it. We are all thought managers, but the way in which we choose to manage our thoughts varies somewhat from person to person.

For example, some people adopt a laissez faire approach to thought management that is characterised by minimal intervention in their own thought processes. This may be rooted in a failure to recognise the power one has over one's own thoughts, and can result in people seeing themselves as helpless victims of their own state of mind. Such people talk as though their thoughts were experiences that just happened to them, rather than experiences they were creating. It's perfectly possible that you may have thoughts you do not want, but the fact remains that the ideas you generate in your mind are your ideas. Your thoughts are just that: *your* thoughts.

In contrast with laissez faire approaches that undermine psychological fitness, active thought management that develops and maintains helpful thinking, will maximise mindpower.

Minds generally work better when used. The mind can be stimulated through any activity that requires focussed concentration. Reflection, reading, writing, further education or training, performing or listening to music, engaging in conversation, or doing crosswords, are all examples of activities that exercise the mind. Such exercises can help to improve concentration, reduce memory loss and increase our subjective well being.

In this chapter we are going to look at some of the aspects of thought management that perhaps more than any others contribute to a fit mind: developing and maintaining a helpful thinking style, helpful self-talk, helpful opinions, and the ability to deal helpfully with painful memories.

What's your thinking style?

Thinking style is the tendency to think about things in a particular way. This is something we learn to do. People build thinking habits just as they build habits in other areas of life.

Through their pervasive influence on how we think, and their indirect impact on our feelings and actions, thinking styles can promote or impede our personal development. Some styles, such as a generally positive outlook, tend to facilitate psychological health, whilst others tend to undermine mental fitness.

Prominent amongst unhelpful styles are biases towards negative or anxious thinking. The tendency to think negatively is a common cognitive problem, and in some cases may contribute to depression. If a person typically thinks about things in a negative way, we may say that their thinking style is characterised by negativity. It is the repetition of negative thinking, rather than the identification of a single negative thought, that is important here. Repeated negative thinking suggests a negative thinking style. We are all capable of thinking negatively, but having a negative thought does not necessarily mean that we have a negative thinking style.

Anxious thinking represents another unhelpful style. Here, the person has a tendency to think about things in a fearful way. In line with the uncertainty they feel, the thoughts of anxious thinkers are often expressed as questions, opening with the words, "What if...?" Here are some examples:

- "What if I'm rejected?"
- "What if I fail?"
- "What if I lose my job?"
- "What if the car/plane/train crashes?"

How about you? What is your style? How would you describe the way you typically frame your thoughts from day to day? What is the main characteristic that strikes you as you reflect on your own thought processes?

Stop for a moment now, and write down any adjectives you can think of that seem to describe the way you tend to think. Then put those adjectives together in the form of a sentence that describes your particular thinking style.

Whatever your style is, you may find it helpful to think of your conscious mind as being a little bit like a cinema. As the owner and manager of that cinema, you get to choose what films are shown. The soundtrack that is heard, and the images that are seen on the cinema screen of your mind, are the ones that you have allowed to play. If you do not like the kinds of films that you see and hear playing in your internal cinema, you can make the decision to show a different kind of film, because you are the boss.

With this in mind, take a moment now to think about how you would like your thinking style to be. To make the most of your mind, you need a thinking style that's helpful. Whilst unhelpful styles are often characterised by negativity, anxiety or inappropriately defensive thinking, helpful styles tend to be characterised by a tendency to think about things honestly and positively.

In practice, it may take a little while to change what's showing on the cinema screen of your mind, but the fact that you are the one in authority means that it is your decision that will ultimately prevail. If you decide that you want different words and images, and you take action to change them, after a while that is what you will get. The reason for the delay is that ways of thinking and perceiving that are well learnt need a little time to be unlearnt, whilst new and unfamiliar ways of thinking and imaging need time and practice in order to be learnt.

How would you like to be spoken to?

Talking to oneself is something we all do. Within the privacy of our conscious mind we chat to ourselves daily about all kinds of things. Because it is our own inner world, we can say whatever we like. No one else will hear. We are in charge, and we can choose to say what we please.

The problem is that the capacity to talk to oneself doesn't mean that what is actually said will be helpful. Each of us develops a particular style of self-relating. For example, one person may be consistently self-critical, always putting themselves down and blaming themselves for everything that goes wrong in their life. Another person may be narcissistic, continually praising their own attractiveness and skill. These are just two of a great many possibilities. Arguably, there are as many different self-relationships as there are people!

When you listen to your own self-talk, what do you hear? How would you describe the way in which you generally relate to yourself? Is it supportive, critical, or what? Unless we take the time to evaluate our self-talk, we will never know whether it could be improved.

If you find that your self-talk is negative, inaccurate, illogical, or unhelpful in some way, decide to change your view.

A common bias is that of those who are overly self-critical. If you observe that you are being your own worst critic, it is time to change your position. People sometimes put up with comments from themselves that they would never accept from anyone else. Overly critical self-talk will rob you of both happiness and achievement. By becoming your own friend and talking to yourself in an honest but encouraging way, you will find that things start to look up.

What do you think?

How helpful are your views? I am not referring merely to what you think on specific topics such as politics, sport, or religion, but the judgements you make about your experience moment by moment. As thinkers, we are continually evaluating our experience and making up our minds about things. We naturally and automatically form opinions and attitudes in response to the events we experience.

What you tell yourself about things will influence your subsequent feelings. How does this work? Let's consider an example. Imagine that it's a wet day. Mr X, a golfer, wakes up, sees the rain, and tells himself that it's bad news, because he wants to go and play golf. The result is that he feels frustrated. In contrast, Mrs Y, a gardener, sees the rain and tells herself that it's good news, because she knows that her garden needs the rain. The resulting emotion for her is one of satisfaction. Both Mr X and Mrs Y experience the same event, but each views it very differently, resulting in dramatically different feelings. An example like this helps to illustrate the powerful effect that our perceptions have on our emotions. Change how you think and you will change how you feel.

It's not just emotions that are generated by what we tell ourselves. The judgements we make about things will also influence our subsequent thoughts and actions. Mr X may decide that his day has been ruined (thought), and vent his frustration and anger on his wife and children (action). Mrs Y may think that her azaleas will look particularly good this year (thought), and arrange a garden party for her friends (action).

The message is clear: thoughts shape lives. If you want a fit mind, you need to think helpful thoughts. The way we see things will have all kinds of consequences for us. Our perceptions will influence our subsequent emotions, thoughts, and actions.

Some thoughts will weaken your mental health and strength. These unhelpful thoughts are your enemies. Your task is to identify them early on and reject them, replacing them with views that will increase your mental fitness.

Specific thoughts can be unhelpful for a variety of reasons. Let's take a look at some of the ways unhelpful thinking may be expressed. Before we do, there are two things we should note. Firstly, these are not watertight categories. Secondly, they are just a few of the great many ways in which people may think unhelpfully. They represent some of the common thinking traps that people fall into. As you read, identify which, if any, describe patterns of thinking that you have experienced.

Unhelpful beliefs about oneself

Anti-self thinking: This is viewing oneself negatively when it is inappropriate or unhelpful to do so. Like all unhelpful thoughts about oneself, it may be spoken in the first or second person. For example, "I'm useless," "I'm a horrible person," or, "You're useless," "You're a horrible person." Anti-self thinking should be distinguished from constructive self-criticism. There are times when it's appropriate and helpful to criticise ourselves. For example, if we have done wrong then it is appropriate to tell ourselves so, and to do what we can to make amends. If we have failed in a task it is helpful to acknowledge it. In contrast with constructive self-criticism, where a simple acknowledgement of one's failure is followed by positive steps to change, anti-self thinking is often expressed in repeated self accusations, recriminations, and put-downs.

Self injunctions: This is seeing oneself as having to reach unrealistically high standards of human conduct. For example, "I must always win in everything I do," "I should be the perfect friend, partner, parent, employee, employer," or, "I ought to do everything perfectly." Happiness is often made contingent on the fulfilment of such personal demands.

Exaggerated responsibility: This is blaming oneself for other people's independent actions and for circumstances beyond one's control. It's attributing negative events to one's own deficiencies. For example, "It's all my fault," "I'm responsible for your happiness," or, in the case of some psychotic individuals, "I am to blame for the earthquake, hurricane, flood (or other natural disaster)."

Unhelpful beliefs about others

Incorrect attributions: This is assuming that we know what others are like, what they think about us, or how they will respond to us, without checking that our view is correct. For example, the person who withdraws from others, because they mistakenly think that they are seen negatively by them.

Social injunctions: This is seeing others as having to reach unrealistically high standards of human conduct. For example, "Others must always treat me with great respect," "You should be the perfect friend, partner, parent, employee, employer," or, "You should know what I'm thinking." Like self injunctions, people often link the fulfilment of these social demands with happiness.

Anti-social thinking: This is viewing others negatively when it is inappropriate or unhelpful to do so. For example, the person who's personal development is stuck because they blame others, rather than accept responsibility for their own problems.

Unhelpful beliefs about life

It should be noted that many of these unhelpful beliefs about life can also apply to the way we think about ourselves and others.

Negative thinking: This is viewing life negatively when it is inappropriate or unhelpful to do so. For example, "Nothing good ever happens to me," "Working hard is a waste of time," or, "There's no point getting up today." Negative thinking may be unhelpful, but it is not necessarily inaccurate. For example, it may be true that a project is failing, but little is achieved by continually telling oneself that things are going wrong!

Life injunctions: This is demanding that life yields unrealistically positive outcomes. For example, "Life must provide all the material and financial wealth I desire," "Life should always reward my efforts," or, "Nothing must ever go wrong." As with self and social injunctions, the attainment of such outcomes is often made a prerequisite for happiness.

Catastrophising (sometimes referred to as magnification or exaggeration): This is making extreme judgements that emphasise the most unpleasant consequences possible in any given situation. For example, an anxious person planning a holiday may dwell on the possibility of being killed in a plane crash.

Selective abstraction: This is selecting one aspect of a situation to focus on, whilst neglecting other aspects. For example, the performer who selectively attends to one unfavourable review, while ignoring the positive reviews of many other critics.

Personalisation: This is overestimating the degree to which specific events are related to us. For example the traveller who, when his train is delayed, invariably treats it as a personal attack on himself.

Arbitrary inference: This is drawing conclusions on the basis of inadequate or inaccurate information. For example, the reader who, seeing an attractive book cover, assumes that the content will be good.

Overgeneralisation: This is making blanket judgements or predictions based on limited evidence. For example, the visitor to a foreign country who experiences bad weather for the duration of their visit, and concludes, "It always rains here."

Polarised thinking: This is interpreting events solely in terms of two opposing and extreme categories. For example, things are seen as, "Black or white," "Good or bad," "Right or wrong," "A success or a failure."

Inaccurate thinking: This is being mistaken in our understanding of things. No mere human has ever been free from the tendency to think inaccurately. All of us, whatever our age, position, or qualifications, will have some inaccurate conceptions about ourselves, about others, or about other aspects of life. The fact that we are unable to acquire perfect knowledge of all things means that getting it wrong is an existential given. Anyone *can* be wrong, and everyone *is* wrong about some things. Some inaccurate beliefs are more unhelpful than others. Unless you are an astronaut, an aircraft pilot, or a sea captain, thinking that the world is flat is unlikely to cause you too many problems, but believing yourself to be invincible will surely get you into trouble sooner or later!

From unhelpful to helpful thinking

Whether the unhelpful thinking that you have identified represents a single idea or an unhelpful thinking style, you may find it helpful to use the following steps as a way of replacing your unhelpful thoughts with new helpful ones. These five steps can help you make the journey from unhelpful to helpful thinking. In order to ensure that they can be easily remembered, the steps have been expressed as a mnemonic based on the word *renew*:

R = Recognise unhelpful thinking

The first step is to recognise when we are thinking in an unhelpful way. The guidelines given in this chapter will help you to do that. If you have not already done so, write down now any unhelpful thoughts that you have identified in yourself.

E = Evaluate unhelpful thinking

The second step is to evaluate the thinking that you have spotted. Why is this thinking unhelpful? Write a brief statement expressing why this particular idea is unhelpful to you.

N = Neutralise unhelpful thinking

The third step is to reject unhelpful thoughts. Try to avoid becoming too focused on those unhelpful thoughts about life, yourself, and others that rob you of time, energy, and happiness, triggering inappropriate emotions of anxiety, anger, guilt, and sadness.

Sometimes unhelpful thoughts can easily be rejected by the mind, but at other times they may be harder to dismiss. If unwanted thoughts are proving resistant to change, this may be because they are well learnt. As you persevere in rejecting them, they will eventually evaporate.

Another possibility is that these ideas are being generated by a particular underlying attitude or issue, in which case you'll need to deal with that attitude, or resolve that issue, before you can get rid of the ideas that come from it. For example, if you are having bad thoughts towards someone whose success you resent, you will find it harder to change these if you fail to deal with the underlying resentment. First change your resentful attitude and then work on the bad thoughts. In most cases you will find it a lot easier this way round.

If you recognise that your thinking reflects an unhelpful underlying attitude, go back to Chapter Three and change that attitude for one that generates helpful thinking. Attitudes represent predispositions to think in certain ways. If your thoughts are being generated by an attitude and you try to change them without addressing that underlying attitude, you will likely find that you get nowhere. In such cases you need to change the attitude behind the thought before you can change the thought itself.

E = Exchange unhelpful thinking for helpful thinking

The fourth step is to replace unhelpful thoughts with new helpful views. Take the unhelpful thoughts that you have identified, and for each one write a phrase or sentence describing a new thought that is more appropriate, more helpful or more positive.

For example, if my unhelpful thinking was, "They won't accept me, so I I'll avoid them," I might change it to something like, "They may or may not accept me, but I probably won't know for sure unless I give them an opportunity. I will approach them, and if they accept me I may gain new friends, but if they reject me I will not let it undermine my self confidence."

Take control of your thinking. Make a radical commitment to seeking and knowing the truth, and to shunning every kind of distorted thinking. Face the negative, but focus on the positive.

W = *Work to establish new helpful thinking*

The fifth and final step is to establish the new way of thinking. This is best achieved by practice. Whenever you catch yourself thinking in the old way, deliberately change your thoughts to the new way of thinking. If you do this every time you become aware of the old thought patterns, you will find that it is only a matter of time before the new thought patterns become an established and automatic part of your thought life.

It's how you tell the story

The ability to remember has the potential to bring us happiness or hurt, pride or guilt, confidence or anxiety. Recalling happy memories can brighten our day, but painful memories may not only trouble the mind, but also exert an ongoing negative influence on our lives in the present. For example, remembering an experience of failure may evoke feelings of anxiety that make us less inclined to try again; remembering a time when we were rejected may unleash painful feelings of hurt, to which we respond with defensiveness and withdrawal, lest we be hurt again.

If you feel that painful memories from the past are holding you back in the present and preventing you from experiencing all that life has to offer, you may need to look at the way you are managing your memories.

The effect that memories have on us is determined largely by what we tell ourselves about them. For example, if I have a memory of being let down by someone I trusted, and I tell myself not only that the damage they did cannot be repaired, but that as a result I will never trust anyone again, I immediately enter a dark place of hopelessness and isolation, from which I may never emerge, unless I change my angle on the story.

I am not suggesting that we pretend black is white. Neither do I advocate denying the horror and pain of bad experiences. It is important to be honest. But I am saying that good memory management is all about how we tell the story. If you can rewrite the story from a more positive angle, without denying or distorting reality, you will come to feel differently about it, and rob the memory of its negative power to pull you down and hold you back.

Let me show you how this works, so that you can apply the principle to your own unpleasant memories. In the example I gave just now, I would take the memory of being let down, and choose a better angle from which to tell the story.

Instead of casting it solely as a tragedy, I might include how I have since coped, despite the wrong done to me, writing the story as one of triumph in the face of adversity. I might also include the valuable lessons I have learnt as a direct result of this experience. Finally, I might include the fact that some people can be trusted more than others, changing the moral of the story from "No one can ever be trusted" to "Find out how much someone can be trusted before you trust them with your resources or your life."

Now the story reads quite differently, despite the fact that it describes exactly the same memory. When I recall the event, I tell myself that although I was disappointed I coped nevertheless, I learnt some valuable lessons, and that as a result I am more careful when it comes to trusting others, checking them out before entrusting them with things that are important to me.

Rewritten, the story becomes more one of success than of failure, and remembered in this more accurate and helpful way, takes me into a place of hope and increased confidence, from which I am better equipped to relate effectively to others.

When you try this for yourself, you may find it helpful to write down the old story and then the new. This can be a lot easier than simply working in your head. You do not need to write a lot – just a few sentences that describe the old and new perspectives. If you like, you can write the old story in the form of a letter to the person in the memory. This is probably not a letter to actually send.

Having written the old version of the story, screw up the paper and destroy it, as a symbol of changing your viewpoint, and as a sign that you are drawing a line under the bad experience.

As for the new story, you may want to hold on to your written copy for a while, so that whenever you remember the incident, you can remind yourself of your new position, thus consolidating your new view so that it becomes your accustomed perspective whenever the memory comes to mind.

6
Take Aim

What do you want?

People are purposeful by nature. They tend to go after what they want.

Desire fulfilled often brings happiness, even if only for a short time, but when expectations are unrealised or goals are unmet, the loss can result in emotions ranging from slight disappointment to severe depression, from mild frustration to violent rage, from minor recriminations to strong self hatred.

If we are going to avoid extreme negative outcomes such as these, we will need to make the most of our motivational mindpower. How to do that is the focus of this chapter.

A motive is, quite simply, a reason for doing something. Motivation is the enthusiasm or need to do something. It is the drive to do what is important to us and to obtain the objects and outcomes we desire, or believe will meet our needs.

Motivation strongly influences both our inner experience and our outer behaviour. It gets people moving, or stopping! It fuels and focuses. It profoundly influences the nature and level of our activity. It channels energy into achieving chosen objectives, and it tends to focus inner experience in line with those objectives. Motivation drives the creation of strategies to achieve its' goals and generates behaviour in line with those strategies.

In this chapter we will be looking at how to develop the kind of goals and expectations that enable the mind to work at its best, what to do when goals and expectations are unmet, and how to identify and change hidden rogue motivators.

If we are going to understand motivation, we first need to know something about the relationship between needs, desires, expectations, and goals.

Needs represent what must happen for us to be healthy
Desires represent what we want to happen
Expectations represent what we think will happen
Goals represent what we will try to make happen

Needs

Needs represent what must happen for us to be healthy. Some needs, such as the need for air, food, and water, are fundamental to our physical health. Other needs are vital to our psychological health and well being, although just what should be included in this category has long been debated by psychologists. Many different psychological needs have been proposed, including the need for stimulation, the need for meaning, and the need for achievement.

When it comes to maximising mindpower, there is one psychological need that perhaps more than any other must be satisfied: the need for truth.

Distortions and deceptions characterise the minds of both the mentally unfit and the mentally ill. Whether systematic or unsystematic, conscious or unconscious, deliberate or unintended, self deception is a powerful enemy of the soul.

The only effective antidote to such distortion is revelation. As light dispels darkness, so truth dispels error. Insight releases the mind from its prison of ignorance.

How is such insight obtained? By making a radical commitment to seeking and knowing the truth even where that truth may challenge us, be inconvenient for us, or be unwelcome to us. The first step to motivational mindpower is acknowledging this fundamental need of the mind, and determining that within ourselves we will pursue the truth, the whole truth, and no knowledge but the truth.

Desires or demands?

Desires represent what we want to happen. They may or may not reflect our needs. It would be nice to think that people would always want what was good for them. Unfortunately, experience attests that this is often not the case. Some needs, such as the need to eat, are significant motivators, but others, such as the need to eat vegetables as part of a balanced and healthy diet, may not motivate some people at all!

People sometimes confuse wants and needs, and this is often reflected in their using terms such as desire, want, and need as though they were synonymous. A need may also be a desire, but a desire does not necessarily reflect a need. What we *think* we need is not necessarily what we *really* need!

Whether they reflect needs or not, desires are powerful motivators. We are strongly motivated to satisfy them. Whatever we desire will tend to become our goal. Desires drive goals, and mix with our expectations to influence how we feel.

Our state of mind can be influenced both by the kinds of desire we choose, and the strength of desire we experience. It is self-evident that some desires are more helpful than others. For example, experiencing a desire to help those around us might make us feel like a better person, whereas indulging a desire to avoid situations we find challenging may contribute to feelings of inadequacy.

Strength of desire also affects our state of mind. Generally speaking, the stronger our desire, the more we will be motivated to fulfil it. As desire increases, it claims more of our attention, and progressively greater mental resources will be invested in it. Our thoughts, our feelings, and our behaviour will increasingly reflect our focus on the object of our desire.

Problems often occur when people turn desires into demands. They take something they would *like* to happen, and make it something that *must* happen. For example, one person might say, "I've got to pass these exams," whilst another might think, "I must have respect." Demands may be made of oneself, of others, or of life events, and are expressed by the kind of self, social, and life injunctions that we looked at in Chapter 5.

Demands don't necessarily cause problems, and may in some circumstances be an appropriate response to the needs of the situation, but when we make demands indiscriminately and inappropriately we may soon find ourselves becoming oppressed or even tyrannised by them. Not only that, the emotional fallout when our demands are not met will likely be greater than would have been the case had we adopted a less demanding position.

One of the main problems with inappropriate demands is that they tend to diminish our awareness of choice. If I say, "I must do x," I'm either saying that I don't have a choice in the matter, or that this is a choice I believe I must make. In each case my lack of freedom is emphasised, rather my freedom to choose.

If you find that you have got into a habit of using words like 'must' too often, and you no longer feel as though you have got much choice, ban yourself from using such injunctions for a couple of weeks in order to break the habit. Another good idea is to remind yourself that however much pressure you may be under to act in a certain way, you are still free to choose, and whatever decision you may make, you are still exercising your power of choice.

Realistic expectations

Expectations represent what we think will happen. They form an integral part of our psychological functioning. Without some ability to reliably predict events in everyday life, we would likely experience extremely high levels of anxiety.

Unfulfilled expectations are responsible for much mental suffering. When expectations of desired outcomes are unmet, or when expectations of undesired outcomes are met, people typically experience negative emotions.

One of the major reasons why expectations are not met is that they are unrealistic. Realistic expectations are more likely to be fulfilled than their unrealistic counterparts. Unrealistic expectations are often unfulfilled, leading to the loss of the desired outcome. Much disillusionment stems from people being illusioned in the first place. If we can improve our ability to recognise and reject illusion, we will fare better when it comes to our expectations. Some illusions are given to us, others we create ourselves.

We should therefore make every effort to ensure that wherever possible our expectations are accurate, or at least realistic. How do we know that an expectation is realistic?

Expectations should be based on available evidence. If we are going to reduce the likelihood of unfulfilled expectations, we need to become better at predicting the future. This is not always as difficult as it sounds. In many cases, an honest assessment of the available evidence will enable a realistic prediction to be made.

The aim in forming expectations is to set them at the outcome level, or level of performance, that can reasonably be expected. Whether we are talking about a person, an organisation, a machine, a natural phenomenon, or a culture, we need to ask what can realistically be expected to happen. This involves considering all the evidence available to us, as well as looking at how has this entity has behaved in the past, in similar circumstances. Past performance is often a good predictor of present performance. If we find that we have expected too much, we must bring our expectations down. If we find that we have expected too little, we may raise our expectations.

For example, if you are a shoemaker and you take on an apprentice to learn the art and trade of shoemaking, you do not expect your apprentice to know everything you do by the end of their first day at work! If you did, you would be very disappointed indeed. No, you set your level of expectation at the level of performance that your apprentice might reasonably be expected to achieve. If the apprentice doesn't quite reach that level, you might be a little disappointed, but you are not worried. You simply adjust your expectations to the ability of your pupil, and take it from there. If your apprentice does better than you expected, you are encouraged, and again you adjust your training accordingly. In this case you may be able to train him or her faster than you originally expected.

This is an example of tailoring our expectations to the outcomes that may reasonably be expected. When we do this, we are far less likely to suffer major disappointment, although we cannot guarantee that things will always work out exactly as we predict. Given that the influence of various factors, some or all of which may be outside of our control, often combine to determine the outcome, it is bound to be the case that at times we will be disappointed, sometimes severely so, especially when what was expected was particularly important to us.

The example of the shoemaker also illustrates the need to change our expectations in the light of new evidence. Many people don't do this, but continue to expect an outcome that has become increasingly unlikely. When the apprentice underperforms or overperforms, the shoemaker adjusts his expectations to allow for the new information, either decreasing or increasing his expectations of his student in line with the trainee's demonstrated ability.

When you next look ahead and try to predict an outcome, remember to set the level of your expectation to the level you believe may realistically be achieved.

Achievable goals

Goals represent what we will try to make happen. People pursue aims and goals in line with their desires, and what they believe will meet their needs. The things we desire will tend to become our goals. People have expectations and goals in every area of life: goals for their relationships, goals for their happiness, and goals for their work – to name just three.

Some goals operate at a higher level, influencing most, or even all, of our life, whilst other goals operate more at ground level, such as our specific intentions in any given moment. For example, planning to go shopping, aiming to get through a certain amount of work before lunch, or trying to get the lid off a jar of jam, all represent these moment-by-moment aims.

The goals we choose exert a profound influence both on how we feel and on how we act. How do we choose helpful goals, and what do they look like?

Like expectations, goals need to be realistic. In other words, having assessed the situation as fully as we can, we believe that it is possible to reach the goal. It's important to note that this is not the same thing as saying that we believe we will reach the goal. We may be convinced of success, but this is not a necessary precondition. All that is required is that we believe the goal to be an achievable one. You need goals you can believe in. If you can't believe in your own goals, you will struggle to maintain them.

When you next look at your own goals, check to ensure that you still believe they can be achieved. Your aims need to be realistic, so do a reality check, and then make whatever goal changes are necessary to ensure that your goals remain achievable.

If a goal is realistic, it will generally also be believable, but the converse is not always the case. Sometimes goals are believable but unrealistic. For example, those who made it their goal to abolish the slave trade chose a goal that appeared unrealistic in the socio-economic context of their day, but they dared to believe that it could be accomplished. Many of the greatest human achievements were made by individuals and groups who were willing to adopt audacious goals that others said could never be reached.

One of the greatest keys to achievement is to break bigger goals down into smaller more manageable goals, and then to take them one step at a time. It has been said that even the longest journey starts with a single step. What is that step for you?

You may find that it helps to write down your end goals, the picture of what you are ultimately trying to achieve, the final destination you are seeking to reach, as well as your instrumental goals, the steps you're going to take in your attempt to reach your destination. It may be that you can see all the steps you need to take, but this is rare. In many cases, the later steps are hidden from view at the start, and in some cases only the first step may be visible. Don't let the unknown put you off. If you believe your cause to be right, dare to step out on the path. It is often the case that as each step is taken, so the next step comes into view.

Some people are inflexible, in some cases erroneously believing that there is only one way to reach the destination they seek. Don't fall into the trap of inflexibility, but be ready to change your plans as necessary. With each step towards your final goal, you may learn more, and this information may influence your next steps. Be flexible, and change your plan as often as you need to, in order to give yourself the maximum opportunity of achieving your ultimate goal. The journey is often very different to what the traveller expects.

Whenever you take another step towards your ultimate goal, recognise the achievement by pausing to celebrate, even if only for a moment! Stop and congratulate yourself (and any others involved in the project), smile, and press on.

Our goals should be driven by our principles and values. If they are not, we are in danger of suddenly realising someday, perhaps towards the end of life, that we have invested our life in something we did not really believe in, creating a state of deep regret that we failed to evaluate our priorities earlier in life.

What is driving your goals? Decide what you want to live for, the things that give your life meaning and purpose. Build your goals around these things. Have achievable goals that you are working towards, and take it one step at a time. Set realistic goals and maintain hope for their fulfilment.

Go for principled purpose. Do the things you believe in.

Keep hope alive, or hold a funeral

In the pursuit of any significant aim, it is not unusual to reach a point where it may seem as if all hope of reaching the desired goal is lost. In reality the situation may or may not be as hopeless as it seems.

Hope is a very valuable psychological commodity. Sustained by hope, people may overcome the greatest obstacles that stand in their way, but without it, the same people may capitulate in the face of the smallest difficulties.

Whatever your goals, you need to believe that it is possible for you to reach them. Otherwise you will find it difficult, if not impossible, to continue working for them. Hope is like a light, illuminating the soul. When the light of hope is extinguished, it leaves only the darkness of grief, depression, or despair. Whilst you have hope that you may reach your desired destination, you will continue the journey, but should your hope die, you will struggle to continue along that path. Why should you, if you no longer believe it is possible?

The presence or absence of hope does not necessarily reflect the reality of the situation. Just as it is possible to have hope in a situation that is hopeless, it's also possible to lose hope when an outcome is achievable. The reason for this is that hope is based on our perception of events, which may be more or less accurate. If we think it cannot be done, it might as well be true, for hope will evaporate. By the same token, if we believe it can be done, hope will burn brightly, even though in reality our cause may be futile.

Often when people feel that a situation is hopeless, instead of stepping back and appraising whether this is really the case, they make an instant reaction, in many cases giving up, believing that they are defeated. Stopping to assess the situation can help to reduce the chances of giving up too soon, or of carrying on when the cause really is futile.

When you next find yourself in a situation of this kind, do what you can to appraise the situation. Try to be objective as you look at the available evidence, but don't restrict yourself merely to observable data. Draw on your past experience, draw on your training, and listen to your gut feelings, your intuition. All these, and other sources of knowledge, can help you make your assessment.

If your assessment suggests that you are still in with a chance, you should keep hope alive and continue to pursue your goal, but if it is clear that the goal can no longer be reached, then you need to come to terms with this. For example, if someone dies, all attempts to revive them having failed, the next step is to hold a funeral and dispose of the body. It is no good propping them up and waiting for them to say something. It isn't going to happen. If something has gone, and cannot be got back, let it go. If a goal truly is hopeless, nothing will be achieved by continuing in pursuit of it. We need to recognise that it's over, grieve where appropriate, and then make new plans.

Sometimes, despite our best efforts to assess what is possible, it is difficult or impossible to tell whether we still have a chance of success. In such circumstances it may be unwise to concede defeat, as we are in danger of giving up prematurely. As a friend of mine says, "It's not over till it's over."

What's your invisible problem?

What do you do when you know something is wrong, but you just can't work it out?

It's not uncommon for people to work consciously and deliberately on their goals, as they seek to develop themselves, their relationships, or their careers. But sometimes despite their continued attempts and best efforts, the desired outcomes, although realistic, remain elusive. Having worked hard to improve things, they cannot understand why the problems remain, and they may feel as if they are 'going round in circles' getting nowhere. The same things keep happening again and again, but they don't know why. They try hard to change things, but each time history seems to repeat itself.

One of the most common causes of such repeated failure is the operation of unconscious strategies and goals. There's more to the mind than meets the inner eye. Whilst some of our aims and expectations are highly visible to us, others are less so, with some completely hidden from consciousness. Moreover, the goals that give their owners the most trouble often lie buried in the unconscious. Because of this, any analysis of goals that looks only at what's above the surface of consciousness is bound to be at best limited.

Unlike their conscious counterparts that are easily accessed, these hidden purposes can be difficult to find. If we're going to more fully understand our own motivation, or help others understand theirs, we need to plumb the unconscious.

There is a reason for these self defeating cycles, but that reason is hidden in the unconscious. It is only when these hidden causes are seen, that their originators can break free from them. Until then they remain trapped in an invisible prison. But when the invisible is made visible, it can be effectively addressed. If you don't know what's causing the problem, you won't know what to do to sort it out.

Because of the damage caused by unhelpful unconscious strategies and goals to psychological health, it is imperative that people-helping resources address this fundamental area, and that caring professionals such as coaches, counsellors, and psychiatrists, have a basic understanding of how to deal with these hidden obstacles to psychological fitness.

In dealing effectively with unconscious influences of this kind, we face two challenges. The first is to make the unconscious conscious. We want to know what the secret mechanism is that is confounding our best plans and efforts. The second is to remove or disable that mechanism.

How do you make the unconscious conscious, or to put it another way, how do you see the unseen? One of the most straightforward ways of doing this is to look at the observable or reportable effects of the unconscious mechanism. Just as apples come from apple trees, and acorns from oak trees, so the consequences of hidden goals and strategies point to the nature of those mechanisms. Although not directly visible, unconscious goals may be inferred from the emotions and behaviour arising from them.

This is good news for anyone who wants to discover what's going on behind the visible scenes of consciousness. In order to discover what we cannot see, we start by looking at what is plainly visible: the actions we take and the feelings we experience. Each can give us helpful clues as to what our hidden goals may be. From these clues we make our best guess as to what may be going on, or to put it in more scientific terms, we build a hypothesis to describe what is happening. Then we test our theory to see whether it is correct.

Try it on yourself. Think of a situation in your own life where things are going wrong but you don't yet understand why. Perhaps you have a partial understanding but you do not have the full picture.

Look at two things. Firstly, describe your own behaviour. What are you doing in this situation? Try to be as honest and as objective as you can be. There might be a number of things that come to mind, so you may find it easier to write them down. Then take them one at a time and make your best guess as to what might be prompting you to act in this way. Asking the following questions may be helpful:

- What might I be telling myself at the back of my mind?
- What belief might lead me to act like this?
- What fear might prompt me to act in this way?
- What goal might be driving this behaviour?
- What strategy might explain these actions?

Secondly, describe your emotions. What do you feel in this situation? Again, be honest and make a note of what you are aware of. Next, take each emotion and make your best guess as to what might be making you feel like this. Ask yourself:

- What might I be telling myself at the back of my mind?
- What belief might lead me to feel this way?
- What unmet goal may be fuelling these emotions?
- What failed strategy might be generating these feelings?

Based on the inferences you have made from your observations of yourself you should now have one or two hunches as to what you think might be going on beneath the surface of your consciousness. Here are some examples of hypotheses based on observation: a socially withdrawn and anxious person may be driven by an unconscious fear of rejection; a workaholic may be motivated by an unconscious goal of approval; an angry and aggressive person may be following an unconscious strategy of projecting blame onto others rather than taking personal responsibility for their actions; and so on.

The test of the hypothesis is you. When you see what is happening, you may or may not like what you see, but there will be a sense of rightness about it, a kind of peace. How quickly you reach this place will vary from one situation to another. On occasions you may get there very quickly, even immediately, with your first hunch proving accurate. At other times you may get there by degrees, starting with a guess as to what's happening which you live with for a while, refining it, or even replacing it, as you continue to think things through.

When you have got a sense of what you think the unconscious influence might be, the next step is to change it. Now that you have something conscious to work with, whether it is a belief, an emotion, a goal, or a strategy, you can use the methods described in the relevant sections of this book to change it for something more helpful.

Go to work on whatever has come to light. Set out to change the influence you believe is operating. As you do, you may find that you learn more about the hidden purposes that influence you. Put this new insight to work, using it to expand your understanding and to inform the changes you need to make.

I hope that you will decide to adopt this technique as part of your lifestyle, regularly looking beneath the surface of consciousness, and working constructively with whatever you can see. There are other ways of exploring the unconscious that take us beyond the scope of this book, but the method described here, if consistently applied, has the potential to develop your mindpower to a level far higher than that which is possible by conscious means alone.

Don't just sit there, do something!

By nature some people prefer to act rather than to plan. They have a tendency to act first, and then (maybe) reflect later. But others are inclined the opposite way, preferring planning to acting. Their tendency is to plan, and to continue planning, perhaps without ever translating their plan into action.

If you are in the first group, you may need to push yourself to plan. Use what we have already covered in this chapter to help you set realistic goals and expectations for your life. If you are in the second group, you may need to push yourself to act. This section will likely be especially relevant to you.

It is one thing to make a decision, but another thing to put it into practice. Setting good goals is, of course, only the first part of the process. Without action, goals remain goals. However good the goals may be, they only become achievements when acted upon.

Sometimes people never get past the first step. They set a goal, but fail to act on it. If you're in this position, ask yourself what is holding you back. Once you have identified the obstacle, you can work on removing it.

Be open to the possibility that you may be citing obstacles as excuses to avoid taking action. If this is so, you need to look at why you're making those excuses. It may be that you are afraid to take the step. One of the most common reasons why people fail to implement their goals and enjoy the satisfaction that comes from constructive achievement, is that they are afraid to take the steps required to translate those goals into reality.

If that's you, be honest with yourself about what you are afraid of. Identify the source of the anxiety. Then use the tools described in Chapter 7 to help you manage that anxiety and move forwards despite it.

Another reason why people sometimes fail to pursue their goals is that they spend too long planning the journey. Some want to know everything that will be involved, before they set out towards the goal. Whilst this might be a very sensible policy in some areas of life, such as making a proper estimate before you engage on building work, or finding out what is involved before you agree to major surgery, it is rarely possible to do this in relation to most life goals.

Detailed quantification and prediction can work well in fields such as engineering or mathematics, but it doesn't work so well in other areas. As a general principle it is good to 'count the cost' but don't try and work out all the detailed steps that you will need to take in order to reach the goal. This is usually not possible, and if you attempt it, you may wait forever, or become so overwhelmed by the magnitude and uncertainty of the task that you give up before you have even begun!

Don't become a collector of unfinished projects. Look at what is holding you back and deal with it. Be honest about real obstacles. These need to be identified and removed. But do not tolerate excuses from yourself. Bin them immediately, face your fear, and do it!

7
Change the View

How do you feel?

The same capacity to feel is capable of lifting us to the heights of ecstasy, or plunging us into the abyss of despair. Mastered, the power of emotion can help drive personal development, but left raw and unharnessed, the same power threatens us with potentially destructive consequences.

Like other functions of mind, the capacity to feel requires effective management if it is to play its part in maximising mindpower. Passion must join with self-mastery if dysfunction is to be avoided and psychological well being gained.

The way we handle our emotions affects our psychological fitness. For example, if you bury your anger you may find it escaping uncontrollably at unpredictable and inappropriate moments; if you are overly self critical and you feed emotions of self hatred you may become depressed or engage in self harm; if you cultivate feelings of jealousy and resentment towards others you may find that this seriously undermines your ability to build healthy relationships.

We have the capacity to experience a wide spectrum of emotions. In fact, the range of feeling that it is possible for an individual to experience is so vast as to defy exhaustive description. For example, if we were able to search all the fiction ever written, listing words and phrases relating to emotion, we would have a large collection indeed!

Despite the great variety of emotional experience, it is possible to identify broad categories of problem emotions. We will be looking at how to deal effectively with these in this chapter, as well as how to increase our experience of positive emotions. But before we do, we need to take a brief look at some of the different ways in which people respond to their own feelings.

Dwelling on how you feel

A common way of responding to our own emotions is to dwell on how we feel. Whilst it is generally helpful to face our problem feelings so that we are aware of them, and can then take appropriate action to resolve or manage them effectively, it's rarely helpful to immerse ourselves in negative or painful emotions. In contrast, dwelling on positive feelings will generally increase our psychological fitness and make us happier people. It is helpful to face negative or painful emotions, but not to feed on them!

Suppressing how you feel

Another option is to suppress how we feel. It may be that we do not want to experience certain feelings at this moment, so we put these feelings to one side. The feelings are pushed just out of consciousness, but we can recall them at any time. There are times when this can be a very helpful response. For example, if you have just been upset by someone, and you then have to perform a delicate and complex task, the ability to lay your feelings aside for a moment may enable you to complete the task successfully, without being unduly influenced by emotion. Having completed the task you may then bring these feelings back to mind in order to deal with them properly.

Repressing your emotions

A more forcible response to our own feelings is to repress them. Again, we push our feelings out of consciousness, but this time we bury them more deeply, so that they cannot easily be recalled. If we experience something that we find really frightening or threatening, one way of coping with it is to bury what we feel. There may be occasions when this dramatic reaction might help us cope with a traumatic event, but generally it is an unhelpful response that puts us out of touch with key aspects of ourselves, and can result in our being unable to be who we really are.

People sometimes confuse repression with healthy self control, thinking that by burying their emotions they are exercising a helpful self discipline. Nothing could be further from the truth. There are times when it is helpful to reign in the expression of emotion, and times when it may be helpful to suppress how we feel, but for the most part repression represents an unhealthy form of self control that undermines psychological fitness. Whenever you repress something, instead of dealing with it effectively in consciousness, the repressed issue will remain unresolved, and, hidden from your view, will continue to exert a negative influence upon you, biasing both your experience and your behaviour in unhelpful ways.

Expressing your emotions

Expression represents a behavioural response to our emotions. Sometimes when we express how we feel, we feel better, if only for a while. Emotional expression can be helpful in releasing pent up emotions, but if the feelings have underlying causes, these will need to be dealt with, if the troublesome emotions are to be resolved.

Continued emotional expression without resolution can lead to the development of negative learnt patterns of behaviour. For example, an angry person who finds relief through regularly expressing their anger, without dealing with its causes, may find that after a while anger becomes their automatic response. In this case, far from improving the well being of the person, repeated expression of the emotion has made matters worse. Such responses can prove devastating to relationships.

If we feel that it is appropriate to express our emotions, we should take care to ensure not only that we deal properly with any underlying issues, but that we express our feelings in a way that is not injurious to others.

Learning from how you feel

The most positive way to respond to our own feelings is to learn what we can from them. If you wish, you may use your feelings to promote your personal development. Your emotions can tell you a great deal about yourself. Whether positive or negative, pleasant or painful, weak or strong, emotions are helpful indicators both of how you see things, and of your underlying attitudes, beliefs, and goals. By monitoring your emotions and learning from them, it becomes possible to advance your own emotional health.

Because they are generally so much more detrimental to our well being than their positive and pleasant counterparts, it is particularly important that we learn how to identify and change negative and painful emotions.

The steps to becoming free from inappropriate negative feelings and to managing painful but appropriate emotions better, are memorably expressed in what I call the *FREE* formula:

F	=	*Face it, don't feed it!*
R	=	*Recognise the event*
E	=	*Explain how you see it*
E	=	*Exchange your view for a better one*

The first step is to face how you feel. If you are used to ignoring your own feelings, this will take a little practice. You may find it helpful to spend five minutes a day writing down how you feel in a journal. This can help you to release pent up emotions. The key is to face the feeling but not to indulge it (unless of course it is a healthy, positive, and pleasant emotion). When we feed on negative and painful emotions they tend to grow, and combined with associated patterns of thinking, can become major complexes that dominate the emotional climate of the mind.

The second step is to identify the event that has triggered the emotion. This may be an external event (e.g., something has gone wrong at work), or an internal event (e.g., you have just remembered something unpleasant from your past). It may be a real event (e.g., you lose something of value), or an imagined event (e.g., you fear losing something of value).

Thirdly, you need to know what you are thinking about the situation. Your answer to this step will show you precisely why you feel as you do. How you see things will determine your emotional response. Discover what you are telling yourself about the outcome, and you have the key to changing how you feel.

The final step is to change your view for a better one. When an artist paints a picture or a photographer takes a photo, they choose the best angle from which to depict their subject. That is exactly what you need to do if you wish to gain mastery over your emotions, rather than have your emotions master you. This may involve reminding yourself of helpful perspectives or truths that you have forgotten, as well as making changes to underlying attitudes, beliefs, and goals.

In the following pages we will be looking at how we can apply these principles to manage some of the most troublesome negative emotions.

Anxiety and threat

Imagine an unlikely scenario. If as you read this page, a hungry lion appears at your side, looks you in the eye, growls, and licks its lips, you will likely feel anxious. The next thing you will probably do is take whatever action you can to survive the encounter. Unlikely though most of us are to ever have an experience of this kind, it does illustrate the survival value of anxiety!

Anxiety is the emotion that alerts us to danger. Without it, our ability to respond to threats would be severely compromised. Anxiety, as a healthy concern, has helped countless individuals and groups to deliver themselves from danger, injury, and loss.

But there is a problem with anxiety and it is this: anxiety can be inappropriate. It is possible to feel more anxious than is warranted by the threat, to feel less anxious than warranted, or to feel anxious when there is no threat at all. It is as though we have an anxiety meter, and when that meter gives us a false reading, our thinking and behaviour can be adversely affected.

In order to understand why this happens, we need to look at the psychological mechanism by which anxiety is generated. Anxiety is an emotion we typically feel when we perceive that something we value is threatened. Whilst we are sure that all is well in the area concerned, we will not experience anxiety in relation to it, but should we become uncertain that all will be well, anxiety is the natural consequence.

The paragraph you have just read contains a key to understanding why we experience inappropriate and unhelpful anxiety. That key is found in the word 'perceive'. How we see the situation will play a major role in determining what we feel about it. If we think that we may be attacked and eaten by a lion in the middle of Paris, we will be anxious, even though the likelihood of such an event actually taking place in that city is very small indeed!

This rather unusual example illustrates how it is not just inaccurate thinking that causes emotional problems. Our perceptions may be accurate yet unhelpful. If I say "I may be eaten by a lion," this is an accurate statement of possibility. However small the chances might be, there *is* a remote possibility of it happening. Some of the dysfunctional thinking that lies behind fears and phobias is based on a faulty assessment of likelihood. Just because a thing *can* happen, it doesn't mean that it *will*. Take our example of being eaten by a lion. It's possible, but it's not probable, at least in Paris.

Free from inappropriate anxiety

At this point I would like to encourage you to make a list of your anxieties, those that you are aware of. Now select one of those concerns to work with, as we consider the steps to effective anxiety management. The method expressed by the *FREE* formula is helpful both for removing inappropriate anxiety and also for managing appropriate anxiety.

F   =   *Face it, don't feed it!*

The first step to beating anxiety is to face it. Do that with the anxiety that you have chosen. Confront your fear and acknowledge how you feel, but do not dwell on anxious thoughts and feelings. Not only is this unhelpful, it usually makes things worse.

R   =   *Recognise the threat*

Secondly, recognise the threat. The kind of event that evokes anxiety is one that is seen as threatening in some way. Take your anxiety and identify what is being threatened, and how. What could you lose? What is under threat here? What valued object, person, state, goal, or outcome, is in real or potential danger? For example, someone anxious about their health might answer, "My health is under threat." A person worried about money might say, "My ability to pay the mortgage/rent is under threat." Someone who is anxious about leaving the house might say, "My life/safety is under threat."

E   =   *Explain how you see it*

Thirdly, listen to what you are saying to yourself about it. Identify your perception. What are you telling yourself about this situation and its outcome? What is your perception of this threat? How do you see it? For example, the person worried about their health may say, "I'm telling myself that I've got a serious illness." The person anxious over money may say, "I'm telling myself that I won't be able to afford it." The person fearful of leaving the house might say, "I'm telling myself that I might get knocked down."

E   =   *Exchange your view for a better one*

Fourthly, find a better view. This may not be easy, but in many cases it *is* possible. Change what you are telling yourself and you change how you feel! Your new perspective should be the most helpful view you can take. It should reflect an accurate assessment of the facts, as well as an accurate assessment of the possibility and the probability (likelihood) of the feared outcome happening. What are the known facts and probabilities in this situation? Tell yourself the truth, as far as you can ascertain it. Then, based on your new perspective, take any practical action that may be required to deal with the threat.

Again let's look at some examples. When the person with health anxieties looks at the facts, they may say, "I only have cold symptoms," or alternatively, "I have been diagnosed with cancer." Telling yourself that you are seriously ill when you've only got cold symptoms is likely to make you unnecessarily anxious. Telling yourself that you are seriously ill when you've been diagnosed as having cancer is accurate, and will generate an appropriate level of concern.

When the person who is worried about their finances looks at the likelihood of being able to pay, they may say, "I've never failed to make the payment yet" (fact), and "I should have enough money, if I budget carefully." In other words, success is not guaranteed, but past experience and careful accounting suggest there is a reasonable likelihood that things will work out ok. Telling yourself that you will not be able to afford it when you have always demonstrated your ability to pay is likely to make you unnecessarily anxious. What if the situation is more serious? For example, the person might say, "I have just been declared bankrupt." Telling yourself that you will not be able to afford it when you have been made bankrupt is likely to be true, and lead to an appropriate level of anxiety.

The person who is afraid to leave the house, and thinks, "I might get knocked down," is thinking accurately. Some people do get struck by motor vehicles. Like so many of the fears that oppress humanity, this anxiety reflects a real possibility. By dwelling on this possible but unlikely negative outcome as though it were likely, the person may become so anxious that they are unable to leave their home, or can only do so with great difficulty. When such a person looks at the facts and probabilities, they may say, "People do get knocked down, but it is unlikely that I will be, especially if I am careful when crossing roads." This is a much more helpful view of the same situation, and will contribute to reduced anxiety.

Anger and frustration

Returning to the unlikely scenario that introduced the section on anxiety, let us imagine that you are a professional photographer on an expedition to gather photos of lions in their natural habitat. This time, instead of turning up and looking hungrily at you, the lion does not appear at all! Your goal to take lion photos is thwarted, and you feel angry.

Anger is the emotion that alerts us to frustration. When what we want to happen is blocked, we typically experience anger. Like anxiety and other emotions, anger can be inappropriate. You may feel more or less angry than is warranted by the frustration, or you may feel angry when there is no real block at all.

How does anger work? Anger is an emotion we typically feel when we perceive that an outcome we value is frustrated. Whilst we see that the way is open to our expectations being met, our goals reached, and our hopes fulfilled, we will be unlikely to experience anger in relation to it, but should we see that the realisation of these is blocked, anger is the natural consequence. Again, the key to understanding exactly why we feel as we do is found in the way we see things.

Free from inappropriate anger

Just as you did for anxiety, make a list of the things that make you angry, and select one of these to practice on, as we work through the steps to effective anger management. Again, we will be using the *FREE* formula to help remove inappropriate anger and better manage appropriate anger.

> F   =   *Face it, don't feed it!*

We have seen that the first step to beating any unpleasant emotion is to face it. So take the example of anger that you have chosen, and allow yourself to experience the emotion. Remember not to feed your angry thoughts and feelings, as this will generally make them worse.

> R   =   *Recognise the frustration*

Secondly, recognise the frustration. The kind of event that evokes anger is one that is seen as blocking the fulfilment of your desires in some way. Take your anger and identify what is being frustrated, and how. What is blocking you? Who or what stands in your way? What valued state, goal, or other outcome, do you think is being hindered or prevented? For example, someone angry about losing a contest might answer, "I was prevented from winning by a better contestant." A person angry over being let down by their best friend might say, "My desire to have a friend I can trust has been frustrated." Someone who is angry over not being promoted might say, "My promotion was blocked."

> E   =   *Explain how you see it*

Thirdly, listen to what you are saying to yourself about it. Identify your perception. What are you telling yourself about this situation and its outcome? What is your perception of this block? How do you see it? For example, the person angry about losing the competition might say, "I'm telling myself that I need to win in order to feel good about myself." The person angry over being let down may say, "I'm telling myself that I shouldn't be treated like that." The person angry over missing promotion might say, "I'm telling myself that I deserve to be promoted."

E   =   *Exchange your view for a better one*

Finally, take a better view. This is where you change what you are telling yourself in order to improve how you feel. Remember that your new perspective should be the most helpful view you can take and reflect an accurate assessment of the facts.

When the angry competitor looks at reality, nothing can change the fact that they lost, but there is something they can change: how they view the situation. Instead of saying, "I need to win in order to feel good about myself," they may choose to change their mind about what is important for self esteem. The result is a new view, expressed by a thought like, "I'm disappointed at losing, but I don't need to win in order to feel good about myself. I feel good about myself because I did my best." Such a view should dramatically lower the level of anger.

In the case of the person who is angry over being let down, it may be true that this was no way to treat a friend, but dwelling on it is not helpful, and is likely to increase the anger felt. Instead of saying, "I shouldn't be treated like that," this person might change both their view of their friend and perhaps also their understanding of trust. This result may be a new perspective expressed by the thought, "My friend should not have treated me like that, but I have learnt how far I can trust them, and that is helpful. I am bringing my expectations of my friend down to the level I can trust them at. I will look for a friend I can trust more, but I recognise that no one is completely trustworthy, and from now on I will only trust people to the level of trustworthiness they have demonstrated."

The person in the third scenario is angry over being bypassed for what they believe is the promotion they deserved. Whether it is true or not that they deserve promotion, dwelling on the idea that they have been undeservingly turned down is unhelpful and will likely sustain bad feelings rather than resolve them. In order to reduce their anger, this person might change their view to something like, "I believe I have what it takes to do the job, and that my employer made a mistake in not promoting me, but I have learnt from this experience, and I will put what I have learnt into practice, as I continue to seek a position that better reflects my abilities and skills."

Sadness and loss

Determined not to be defeated, you plan a further expedition to photograph lions. This time, your best friend expresses a strong interest in coming to, and you agree to travel together. But unfortunately, while you are sleeping, a lion comes and eats your friend.

Sadness is the emotion that alerts us to loss. When we see that something we value is lost, we typically experience sadness. Whether it is a lost object, a lost person, a lost opportunity, or a lost hope, we will grieve to a greater or lesser extent. Like other emotions, sadness can be inappropriate. You may feel more or less sad than is warranted by the loss, or you may feel sad when there is no real loss at all.

Again, the key to understanding lies in identifying how we see things. If we see that what we value is under threat and may be lost, we will tend to become anxious, but if we believe that the thing we value *is* lost, we will be sad.

As a general rule, the depth of sadness experienced will tend to be in proportion to the importance we attach to the object or outcome. For example, if I lose a pen I particularly like, I may feel slightly sad, but if a close friend dies, my feelings of grief will be much stronger.

Hope is the element that keeps sadness at bay. Whilst we have hope of keeping or of obtaining what we value, we will not be sad, but should we lose that hope and become convinced that the valued object or desired outcome is lost, we will probably experience sadness.

The kind of sadness we experience will be to a large extent determined by the nature of our relationship with what we've lost. If we value the object or outcome that has been lost, we will grieve. If, however, we also believe that it is imperative for us to have it, its loss will tend to elicit the particular kind of grief reaction that we call reactive depression. As the name suggests, this state represents a certain type of reaction to loss.

In this reaction there is a double loss of hope. Not only does the person lose hope of keeping or obtaining what they value, but in addition they lose hope for the future. However deep a grief may be, if the griever believes there is a future without the lost object, they may be very upset, but they are not likely to become depressed. But if they have told themselves that they *must* have it, they cannot have it, and there is no hope for life without it, they will likely prove a candidate for reactive depression. So it is that hope plays an important role in influencing whether a person will simply experience normal grief, or whether they will become depressed following a perceived loss.

Free from inappropriate sadness

In the same way that you listed some of your anxieties, and some of the things that make you angry, make a note of any feelings of loss that you are experiencing at this time in your life. Select one to work on, as we look at the steps to managing sadness. As before, we will be working with the *FREE* technique, in this case to remove inappropriate sadness and improve our management of loss.

F = *Face it, don't feed it!*

Take the feeling that you have selected and face it. Allow yourself to feel whatever emotions come to mind. Then, after experiencing the emotions for a short while, move to the next step. If you have experienced a significant loss you will need to grieve, so don't bury your feelings. At such times you may find it helpful to be with others, although you may not feel like doing a lot of talking. Feelings of grief often come in waves. Allow yourself to feel the pain when it comes, but be careful not to magnify it by dwelling continually on your loss or by taking an exaggerated view of how bad things are.

R   =   *Recognise the loss*

Secondly, recognise the loss. The kind of event that evokes sadness is one that is seen as losing you something or someone you value. Take your feelings and identify what has been lost, and how. What valued person, object, state, goal, or outcome, have you lost? For example, someone who has lost a job might say, "I am unhappy because I've lost my job." A person grieving over the unexpected death of a close friend might say, "I feel devastated at losing my closest friend." Someone whose business is failing might say, "I'm upset because I am losing my business."

E   =   *Explain how you see it*

Thirdly, listen to what you are saying to yourself about it. Identify your perception. What are you telling yourself about what has happened? What is your perception of the loss? How do you see it? For example, the person who has lost their job might say, "I have to do that job, and I cannot see how I could ever be happy not doing it." Such a response is likely to lead to strong grief feelings, or even depression. The person whose close friend has died might say, "I'm telling myself that this is a major loss, but I am grateful for having had such a great friendship. I know that I'll miss my friend, but it won't stop me getting on with my life." This person may be very sad, but they are unlikely to become depressed. The business person might say, "I'm telling myself that it's over and that I'm finished," a view that's likely to elicit strong grief feelings.

E   =   *Exchange your view for a better one*

Fourthly, find a better view. By working on your view of the loss, it is possible to improve how you feel. A new and better perspective that accurately reflects the facts and enables you to maintain hope for the future can help you contain, reduce, and in some cases eliminate feelings of sadness.

In the case of the person who has lost their job, their current view stresses how imperative it is that they have the job in question, and pictures an unhappy future for them without it. The result of such a perspective is likely to be depression. By changing their view, this person may significantly reduce their level of sadness, and avoid depression. For example, they might say, "I'm telling myself that I'll miss my job, but that I'm now free to explore what I'll do next with my time and energy." This new perspective is likely to elicit both a sense of sadness at losing a job they enjoyed, but also a sense of expectation, or even excitement, at the thought of possible new activities and involvements ahead.

The person whose friend has died provides us with an example of a constructive response to loss, but even where the current response is a helpful one, there may still be room for improvement. A good view may not be the best view. Perhaps there are additional positive points that might be included in the view, improving it still further. For example, the bereaved friend might also say, "My friend led a full and rewarding life," or, "The good effects of my friend's life will continue," or, "My life will always be the better for having known my friend."

In cases where the person has mistakenly identified loss, sadness may be removed altogether. Our third example may represent a situation of this kind. The business person who looks at their failing business and concludes that it is over has pre-judged the outcome. The business may be failing, but it has not yet failed. Changing their view to one that better reflects the current state of affairs will help them to reduce, or even eliminate, feelings of sadness. For example, they may say, "My business is going through a difficult time, but I will respond to this challenge by doing everything I can to overcome the current difficulties, improve my business, and develop it for the future." The mixed emotions generated by this kind of response may include feelings of anxiety, confusion, enterprise, and creativity, but not sadness, because at this stage the business has not been lost.

Guilt and wrong

Upset that a lion ate your friend, you decide to photograph tigers instead. You launch a further expedition on which you make new discoveries of tigers in remote regions. However, on your return you learn that you were followed by poachers who have killed a number of them. You feel guilty that your trip has contributed to their death.

Guilt is the emotion that alerts us to our own wrong doing. When we see that we are to blame for something, we typically experience guilt. Like other emotions, guilt can be inappropriate. You may feel more or less guilty than is warranted, or you may feel guilty when you have done nothing wrong.

Yet again, perception is plays a key role in determining how we feel. Whilst we see that we are living in accordance with our own moral principles, we will not experience guilt, but should we see that we have acted contrary to those principles, guilt is the natural consequence. Our perception, or misperception, of our own wrong doing, will influence whether or not we feel guilty, and if so, how guilty we feel.

The role of perception can be seen in the tiger story. If you see that you are responsible for the death of the tigers, you will likely feel guilty, but if you see that the poachers are responsible for their death, you may not feel any guilt whatsoever. In this case, it is true that you are part of the chain of events that led to their death, but it is not true that you killed them. If you take responsibility for the part you played in inadvertently and unintentionally leading the poachers to the tigers, you may feel sad and upset at their loss, as well as anger towards those who killed them, but your feelings of guilt will likely be restrained at an appropriate level.

Free from inappropriate guilt

Just as you listed some of your feelings of anxiety, anger, or sadness, so now I would like to invite you to make a note of any feelings of guilt that you are currently experiencing. Select one of these to work on, as we look at the steps to managing guilt. Again, we will be working with the *FREE* technique, using it to improve our management of guilt and to remove inappropriate or false guilt feelings.

F   =   *Face it, don't feed it!*

The first step to managing guilt is to face it. Do that now with the feeling that you have selected. Allow yourself to feel the emotion. Then, after experiencing them for a short while, move to the next step. Don't over-indulge your guilt feelings.

R   =   *Recognise the wrong*

Secondly, recognise the wrong. The kind of event that evokes guilt is an inner or outer action that we see as violating our moral principles. Take your feelings and identify the wrong. What event has led to your guilt? What have you done? It may be an inward attitude, a thought, a decision, a plan, an outward action that you have taken, or some combination of these.

For example, someone who is jealous of another person's success might say, "I feel guilty because I've been thinking bad thoughts about them." A person whose friend commits suicide might say, "I feel guilty because I failed to prevent my friend from taking their own life." Someone reaching the end of their life might say, "I feel bad that I didn't spend more time with my family and do more for them."

E   =   *Explain how you see it*

Thirdly, listen to what you are saying to yourself about the wrong. Identify your perception. What are you telling yourself about what happened? What is your perception of the wrong? How do you see it? Where have you violated your own moral code?

For example, the person who is jealous of another's success might say, "I feel it's unfair that they have more than I do, but it is wrong of me to think about them like this, and I'll change my attitude." Such a response is likely to lead to appropriate guilt feelings, as well as positive emotions generated by the constructive change of attitude.

The person whose friend committed suicide might say, "I should have stopped my friend from taking their life." A view of this kind is likely to make them feel bad indeed.

The person nearing the end of life might say, "I'm telling myself that I've not lived my life as I should have, that the past can't be undone, and that it's too late to put things right." A hopeless perspective of this kind is likely to elicit strong feelings both of guilt and grief.

E   =   *Exchange your view for a better one*

Fourthly, find a better view. By working on your view of the wrong, it is possible to improve your management of guilt. Your new perspective should be the most helpful view you can take.

In other words, it should reflect an accurate assessment of the facts, as well as an accurate assessment of your responsibility for what happened. Tell yourself the truth, as far as you can discern it, on both counts. Then, based on your new perspective, take any action that may be necessary to put things right (as far as it lies in your power to do so), such as apologising, redressing the wrong, or making restitution.

In the case of the jealous person we see a helpful response that reflects an honest admission of feelings, an accurate assessment of wrong according to their moral values, and a powerful change of attitude. Constructive though this view is, it's possible that there may be an even better perspective! For example, it is possible that by adding the idea that they too are successful, or can be successful, but perhaps in other ways, the view might be improved still further. The new perspective might be, "I felt it was unfair that they had more than I did, but I realised that it was wrong of me to think about them like that, and I changed my attitude. I believe that in my own way, I too am a success/can be a success."

The person who feels responsible for the suicide of their friend may be experiencing inappropriate guilt. If there was nothing they could have done to prevent their friend's action their guilt is entirely unwarranted, a false guilt reaction. Saying, "I should have stopped my friend from taking their life," is an unhelpful viewpoint that will generate guilt where none is deserved. A better view, such as, "I am upset by my friend's death, but it was their decision; there was nothing I could have done to prevent it," will likely free the person from false guilt feelings, and replace them with an appropriate sense of loss.

The view of the person who regrets not spending more time with their family, is part helpful, and part unhelpful. It may be accurate to say, "I've not lived my life as I should have done, and the past can't be undone," but it is not necessarily the case that, "It's too late to put things right." In fact, it may be possible to put a great deal right. Whilst they still live, there is time to talk with other family members, to apologise, to explain, and to ask for and receive forgiveness. A better view might reflect truths of this kind and be expressed as follows: "I regret not spending more time with my family, and I can't change the past, but I can influence the future. I will make time for my family from now on, and I will seek to put things right with each one, explaining, apologising, and asking their forgiveness." Such a view will offset the guilt over the past against the good feelings that result from doing the right thing now.

Keys to feeling good

Because it is such a major contributor to emotional health, the ability to manage painful emotions effectively has been our focus for much of this chapter. Once you have learnt this skill, you can use it not merely with anxiety, anger, sadness, or guilt, but with any other painful feeling, whenever necessary. Practice emotional self management until it becomes an automatic part of your daily life.

Having addressed the challenge of dealing with painful emotions, we will close this chapter by taking a look at some of the most powerful keys to feeling good.

Treat yourself properly and remain true to your principles

Just as you will be happier if other people treat you well, so you will feel better if you accord yourself the same good treatment. If, in addition, you seek to do what is right, and repent when you do wrong, your conscience will support you rather than condemn you.

Think better things

You need to *think* good if you want to *feel* good. We have seen that our feelings are determined largely by what we tell ourselves. Just as anxiety is driven by how we see threats, anger by perceived obstacles, and sadness by our view of loss, pleasant feelings are driven by pleasant perceptions. If you want to experience happier days, think about happier things. Take a better view. Without denying negative realities, choose to dwell on whatever is good, and train your mind through practice to always look at things in this kind of way.

Feed the good feelings and starve the bad

Whilst we should acknowledge but not over-indulge negative and painful emotions, feeding on positive and pleasant ones not only strengthens good feelings, but can contribute to increased psychological fitness. Savour positive emotions that flow from positive thoughts and memories. Enjoy them.

Express the positive in how you act

How we act can influence how we feel. Choose to act down, and it may not be long before you (and possibly those around you!) start to feel down. Wearing a frown, adopting an unfriendly manner, expressing negative attitudes, and making critical comments are all examples of actions that will neither inspire you nor anyone else.

Take an honest look at your own actions in order to assess the degree to which they express the positive things in your life. I am not suggesting that you pretend everything is fine when it is not. My aim is to help you increase your psychological fitness, not to reduce it through self-deception and dysfunction! Once you have identified the positives in each situation, make sure that they influence how you act. Choose to act positively, and it is likely that both you and those around you will start to feel better.

Wherever appropriate, exchange your frown for a smile, adopt a friendly manner, express positive attitudes, make constructive comments, brighten up your appearance, and laugh.

Do what you can do

Do not bite off more than you can chew. If you take on too much, you will probably find that good feelings evaporate. Decide on what you can do, and then go for goals you can achieve. You will feel better if you are achieving something, especially something that is meaningful to you. To apply this principle, you may need to take your major goals and break them down into achievable steps.

Do more of the things you enjoy

The energising and uplifting effects of doing what you enjoy will extend beyond the events themselves and be felt whilst you are doing other things, including less enjoyable tasks!

Do what you can for others

Look out for ways to help those around you each day. There are many things we can do to encourage and support others. If you are unaccustomed to living this way, you may be surprised at how good it makes you feel!

Trust in God

Fully entrust your life into the hands of a Loving Power infinitely beyond yourself, and you will know a great weight lifted from your soul.

8
Body Building for the Mind

Body and mind

We don't have to look far for evidence of the close link between mind and body. Anyone who has tried to solve a complex problem whilst exhausted, or to remain focused on a dull task when they are hungry and would rather eat, knows how inter-related these two dimensions are.

Because of this close relationship between the physical and non-physical aspects of our being, any work we do on developing one is likely to have a beneficial effect on the other.

In order to make the most of your mind, you must pay attention to your body. By doing what you can to look after your body and to manage its needs in a responsible way, you may not only improve your physical health and fitness, but also increase the power of your mind.

This chapter considers the bodily keys to maximised mindpower. Practice these steps, making them an integral part of your daily life and it will not be long before you begin to observe the beneficial effect they have upon your mind.

Rest and relaxation

Which of the following statements comes closest to your views?

(a) Work first, and rest when you are tired
(b) Rest first, and work when you are rested

Your answer will say something about how you see the cyclical relationship between work and rest.

Rest is the field in which creativity blooms, the foundry in which new ideas are forged, the factory in which strong purpose is generated. In rest, the spirit may be inspired, the mind enlightened, and the body energised. Rest is foundational.

A good night's sleep

Let me ask you two questions. Firstly, "How much sleep do you need in order to be at your best?" Please be precise in your answer. Avoid vague replies such as, "A lot," or, "Not much," but give the number of hours you think you need each night. Secondly, "Are you getting this much sleep each night?"

The first question is important because people differ in terms of how much sleep they need. Most need seven to eight hours a night; some can get by on just a few hours; others need more.

You need to be clear about how many hours sleep you need each night. If you have not already done so, take a moment now to honestly assess your own need for sleep.

Your answer to the second question is important because it may highlight a need for change in your sleep patterns. If you are getting the sleep you need, that's great, but if not, what can you do to rectify the situation?

A good place to start might be to take your diary and reschedule your life and time, so that, as far as possible, you get the sleep you need to function at an optimum level. If you regularly get the sleep you need, you will find that the benefits to both your physical and psychological vitality are well worth the sacrifice of extra hours awake.

Helpful though it is to get the sleep we need, achieving a good night's sleep is not always easy in practice. Even if we schedule enough time for sleep, we may have difficulty sleeping, or feel that, despite having been asleep, we have not slept well.

Various things can disrupt our sleep. Common causes include anxiety (we may be worrying about something), excitement (we may be over-stimulated), depression (we may feel down or depressed over something), or alcohol (we may be drinking too much just before we sleep).

If your sleep is being disrupted by anxiety or other strong emotions, you need to manage these, as best you can, using the principles of emotional self management described earlier in this book.

If you find that you are often too excited to sleep, you may need to look at ways of unwinding beforehand. Spending half an hour or so relaxing before sleep can help you calm body and mind so that you are better able to sleep when the time comes. Reading or listening to peaceful music, are examples of activities that can help you relax. Some find it helpful to avoid watching television just before sleeping, as it is too stimulating.

If you think that depression may be the problem, see your doctor. In addition, do what you can to identify and resolve the underlying causes. You may find the earlier section on *Sadness and Loss* helpful in this respect.

Finally, if you are in the habit of drinking alcohol just before you sleep, you may need to change this. Alcohol is a depressant drug that can prevent you from getting enough deep sleep, so that you feel less refreshed on waking.

Leisure time

What do you do when you are neither working nor sleeping? Take a moment now to briefly describe your leisure time. Include not only what you do, but also how much leisure time you have each week.

Next, I would like you to answer two questions. Firstly, are you getting enough leisure time? As a general rule it's a good idea to have at least one full day off each week. Secondly, how much of your leisure time is spent relaxing? In addition to our need for adequate sleep, we all need time to do things that are relaxing and restful.

If you find that you are not getting the leisure time you need, why not change your lifestyle now? Take your diary and mark one day each week as a day of rest. Then keep to your plan. If you're not used to taking time off you may find this difficult at first, but with practice you will grow to appreciate this valuable key to your well being. Make time for things that you enjoy!

When you assess your own relaxation time, don't mislead yourself concerning what's relaxing and what's not. Not everything that people classify as relaxation is relaxing! For example, visiting theme parks is a recreational activity, but the surge of adrenalin you get from riding a 'death-defying' ride is not relaxing. You may enjoy running marathons as part of your leisure time, and the training required for it may increase your fitness, but running is not relaxing. Relaxing activities are restful, requiring little energy and effort.

If you find that you are not taking time to properly relax, try to find something you enjoy doing that does not involve high levels of concentration or a lot of energy, and when you have found it, make it part of your week. Again, you may find it helpful to enter it in your diary.

Listening to music is a good example of an activity that can be relaxing. Music can have a powerful effect on the mind, relaxing, inspiring, and elevating mood. Play the music that helps you relax.

Peace under pressure

Living in a world of constant change, each of us will experience the reaction we call "stress". Stress is a physical reaction to a stressor. It's an adjustment or coping response, designed to protect and preserve us. A "stressor" is anything which causes stress. It could be a psychological event, such as the belief that people are out to get us, a physiological event, such as injury, or something that takes place in our surroundings, such as caring for a seriously ill friend or family member.

All stress starts with the body's "fight or flight" response. In this reaction, the brain sends messages to the body, preparing it to "fight" the present danger, or "flee" to escape. These messages cause chemical reactions within the body, as it is primed for action with spurts of adrenaline and cortisol.

A certain amount of stress can be good for us. In fact some people complain that life is boring when they lack adequate stimulation of this kind. An appropriate level of challenge can energise us to greater achievement. But too much stress, for too long, can be bad news, leading to fatigue, exhaustion, ill health, and finally mental and physical breakdown.

What's the answer? We need to increase our ability to cope with conflict, crisis and change, the challenges and traumas that make life stressful. In other words, we must learn to effectively manage stress and become more resilient people.

Good stress management involves a range of skills that include the following:

- *Stay true to your core principles*
  If you act contrary to your own beliefs and values, inner tension and stress will be generated.

- *Face problems, but don't feed them*
  Stress is amplified when the mind becomes overly focused on unpleasant facts or negative possibilities. This can be prevented by putting boundaries around negative thinking. You should give sufficient attention to unpleasant facts in order to take effective action, but not dwell on them more than is necessary.

- *Maintain a positive mental attitude*
  However challenging things are, choose to face them from a positive vantage point. By dwelling on whatever is good in the situation, and laughing where appropriate, you will activate a powerful antidote to stress.

- *Set realistic goals and expectations*
  If you set your expectations and goals at an achievable level, and scrap those that are unrealistic, your stress levels will fall.

- *Learn how to manage painful emotions*
  Strong emotions can be stressful, so learn how to deal with them in a healthy way.

- *Breathe deeply*
  Breathing exercises can be helpful in reducing stress. By breathing deeply you can regulate your heartbeat and help keep stress at a manageable level. When you begin to feel stressed, slowly take in a deep breath through your nose, hold it for a moment, and then let it out slowly through your mouth. Continue for a few minutes until you can feel a difference.

- *Relax your muscles*
  Muscle relaxation can also be helpful. By systematically relaxing the muscles of your body when you lie down to sleep each night, you may find that you sleep better and that your body is more relaxed during the day. Go through each set of muscles in turn, tensing and then relaxing them, working up from your toes to the top of your head. Don't be surprised if by the time you get to your head, your feet have tensed up again! You may find that you need to go through the exercise a few times before you remain relaxed.

- *Take regular physical exercise*
  Exercise has been shown to help reduce stress levels, so find a physical activity you enjoy, and schedule it in your diary.

- *Cut back on stimulants*
  Caffeine and nicotine act as stimulants in the body, and may add to your stress.

- *Enjoy relaxing activities*
  Doing what you enjoy will help you win the battle against stress. Have dinner with friends, watch a favourite film, take a relaxing bath or shower, or go for a walk.

- *Listen to music*
  Listening to music may help you stay calm and focused. Be aware that music can influence mood, so choose something that has a calming effect upon you.

- *Remove stressors where possible*
  Sometimes the cause of stress can be removed. For example, you may reduce stress by allowing more time for important tasks. Remember that there is a limit to the amount of stress you can take, so you need to monitor how much pressure you are under, avoiding excessive stress wherever possible.

- *Start the day with a short time of meditation*
  Taking a few minutes to still your mind and refresh your spirit at the beginning of each day can help create a foundation of inner peace from which to most effectively manage the stresses of the day ahead.

Diet and drugs

Both physical and mental health can be influenced by diet. Like the fuel for an engine, or the raw materials used to make a product, the quality of what we eat and drink will have a major effect on the condition and performance of both body and mind.

You need a healthy diet to function at your best. Research has demonstrated the value of a balanced diet for good mental health, and has suggested a direct link between what we eat and how we feel. Here are some suggestions on how to increase your psychological fitness by improving your diet.

You need to eat a certain amount of carbohydrates, as these provide the glucose that gives your brain the energy to think. Eating wholegrain cereals and breads can help increase your mental energy. Carbohydrates can also lift your mood, as they help to raise serotonin levels.

Ensure that you keep to a low-fat, low cholesterol diet, as this will help to keep your heart and blood vessels in good shape and maintain a good supply of oxygen and nutrients to the brain.

Eat generous quantities of fruit and vegetables. The antioxidants they contain are thought to be good for brain cells, and may also help to prevent the build up of plaque in the arteries.

Watch your caffeine intake. Caffeine is a powerful stimulant related to cocaine and amphetamines, and found in a number of plants including coffee beans, tea leaves, and cocoa beans. In addition to being a natural part of products such as coffee, tea, and chocolate, it is often added to other products, including soft drinks, pain medications, and energy products. Too much caffeine can cause agitation, anxiety, panic, headaches, nausea and sleep problems. There is a lot of individual variation in reactions to caffeine. Some people have one cup of coffee and get a range of symptoms, whilst others can drink a number of cups before noticing any effects of this kind. The best thing is to know your own tolerance level, and seek to stay within it.

Avoid excessive alcohol. People often drink alcohol because of the effect it has on the way they feel and their state of mind, but too much alcohol can be bad for your physical and mental health. The long-term effects of drinking too much alcohol include a higher risk of heart disease and stroke, as well as the possibility of brain damage and memory loss. If you drink alcohol, drink sensibly.

Don't smoke. Not only does smoking carry significantly increased risks of cancer and heart disease, but research suggests that it is linked with the appearance of mental health problems such as anxiety and alcohol abuse. Some smokers argue that smoking helps them to cope with stress, but the evidence suggests that smoking might actually cause stress, and that any relief gained from smoking is only short term.

Don't take illegal drugs. Using these to change your own mental state is a dangerous choice that can easily lead to addiction and can undermine both your mental and physical health.

Do take any medication you are prescribed for mental health issues. These problems sometimes have a physiological component, and some mental health conditions respond well to certain drugs.

Finally, whatever your diet is like, don't overeat. Becoming overweight may compromise not merely your physical health and fitness, but adversely affect your self esteem and confidence.

Exercise and activity

The benefits of exercise to health and well being have long been observed. Effective exercise can be undertaken without any specialist equipment or facilities, and its physical advantages include increased suppleness, stamina, and strength.

Suppleness is enhanced by exercises involving stretching, such as reaching down and touching your toes. Simply doing some stretching of the main muscle groups for a minute or two each morning, can help to increase and maintain your suppleness, contributing to optimum mobility as you age.

Stamina is developed through aerobic exercise, such as running, rowing, or brisk walking. Regular exercise of this kind makes us feel better by releasing the body's own chemicals that energise us and lift our mood. It strengthens both heart and lungs, and provides a powerful antidote to anxiety, stress, and depression. By helping the flow of blood and oxygen to your brain, such exercise can help to improve many aspects of cognitive functioning, including problem solving, reasoning, memory, and reaction times.

Some people like to go to a gym, or to take part in an energetic sport, but you do not have to do either of these things to get aerobic exercise. Walking briskly for a few hours each week can provide you with all the aerobic exercise you need. In fact, Hippocrates, the father of medicine, argued that walking was the best medicine.

Even if you are only able to do a small amount of aerobic exercise each day, it is better than nothing. Be on the lookout for small ways of adding exercise to your daily life. For example, if it's a short way, you might decide to walk briskly rather than take the car. If you are going up to the next floor, take the stairs rather than the lift.

If you are not used to taking vigorous exercise, be careful that you do not overdo it at the start. Begin by doing a little, and gradually increase it, until you are regularly getting the level of exercise you need. Choose forms of exercise you enjoy, and aim to get at least thirty minutes of exercise every day, if you can. Some like to divide this into three exercise 'breaks' of ten minutes each.

Strength is increased by building muscles, so it's a good idea to put your muscles to work each day, in a way that is appropriate to your age, existing strength, and state of health. Muscles waste if they are not used, but remain strong if regularly exercised. By simply keeping active you will ensure a reasonable level of muscular strength, but if you want to go beyond this and get stronger, you will need to make greater demands on your muscles, for example by doing resistance training with weights at a gym.

Exercise is not the only kind of physical activity that is helpful to our physical and psychological health. The simple act of getting out in the sun for at least ten minutes each day can increase our serotonin levels, lifting our mood. Socialising, gardening, and exercising, are all examples of activities that can be undertaken outdoors.

9
Ideas in Action

What do you think you're doing?

The things we do are not just an expression of who we are. They shape who we are. We are influenced by our own actions.

For example, if you practice a skill such as cookery until it is well learnt, you become a skilled cook. Similarly, if you practice the skills of maximised mindpower, to the point where you do them automatically and unconsciously, you become a skilled manager of your psychological well being, your own psychological fitness trainer.

In addition to their direct effects, our actions also influence us indirectly via their impact on others. Those around us are influenced by our actions. They build a picture of us, based on their interpretation of what they see us do, and what they hear us say. How they subsequently relate to us will be significantly influenced by this picture.

In this chapter I want to encourage you to look at your behaviour, to develop its potential for increasing your psychological fitness, and to seek to find a good balance between different kinds of behaviour, such as work and play, activity and rest.

Human behaviour is a big field, so we'll be focusing selectively on those aspects that are particularly significant for our psychological fitness.

Recreation

We have already touched on this important area when we looked at the physical need for relaxation and leisure. Recreation, as the English term implies, is to do with getting back our health and vitality. In a life where there are great pressures to work, recreation can easily be squeezed out, but the loss of leisure is always a false economy. However difficult your circumstances or however important your work, recreation should still be a priority. In fact, where there is pressure to overwork, it is all the more necessary that you protect your valuable recreation time.

Small children do not have to be taught to play. It is something enjoyable that they do automatically and instinctively. But as they pass through life, and must wrestle with its challenges and responsibilities, many people lose the sense of fun they once enjoyed.

Fun and laughter are as important for the psychological well being of adults as they are for that of children. A good sense of humour is one of the ingredients of mental fitness. Have you become so serious that you can no longer see the funny side of things? When did you last hear yourself laugh? If you have lost your sense of humour somewhere along the road of life, stop now and lighten up. If it is so long since you last laughed that your jaw is rusty, you can oil it by watching comedy films, or by buying a book of jokes you find amusing, and reading one or more a day.

Doing things we enjoy brings refreshment to the mind as we take a break from the things that usually occupy us. It is like a mini holiday. We stop thinking about the problems and issues that we are working on, and focus instead on something we really enjoy.

Interestingly, this often has the indirect effect of assisting our problem solving, as the mind may come up with new insights, innovative solutions, or creative ideas, during its break. Even if this does not happen, we return to our usual tasks with a mind refreshed and thus better able to work on the issues that confront us.

Take a look at your life and ask yourself whether you are having enough fun. If you are not, it may be time to take action. Start by thinking about what you would like to do. What would you enjoy? If you are really out of practice when it comes to play, you may need to experiment with a number of things before you settle on something.

The key is to do the things you enjoy, the things you feel good doing. As long as they are healthy, and they don't hurt anyone else, these activities will help sustain your optimum functioning. Dine out, watch a funny film, see a play, listen to music, walk on the beach, read a good book, go for a run, talk to a friend, or practice your sport. Play is good for you.

Don't automatically assume that you know what you enjoy. Even if you have got a good awareness of what you like doing, there may be things you have never done that you would love if you did them. Because of this, it's a good idea to try new things from time to time. You may be surprised at what you discover!

In order to make sure that your recreation activity actually happens, you may need to carve out time for it in your diary – and not just for the week you're in. We are talking about a lifestyle here, so you need to ensure that fun time is a regular part of your weekly schedule.

When you do your favourite things, remember not to rush through them so fast that you fail to derive pleasure from them! Take the time you need to enjoy the activity. When it comes to recreation, it is often better to slow down, to take the longer route, to enjoy the space or the silence.

Making space and going slower also means that you have got time to attend to what your senses are telling you. You can stop to hear the birds singing, or to enjoy the delicate fragrance of a flower, or to take in a beautiful view.

Recreation is not just about taking up a hobby, or adopting a new interest. It is also about small but significant actions that can have a restful or restorative impact on us.

Having a change of scene is one such action. A change of scene can improve how we feel and help us to see things more clearly. When we are depressed, anxious, or simply working hard, it is easy to spend long periods in the same place. By taking a break and having a change of scene, the pressure we are under may be eased, and we may return feeling refreshed, or even having obtained a better perspective on things. Going for a walk, moving to another room (or even a different place in the same room), and chatting to friends or colleagues, are all ways of taking a break.

Spending time outdoors is another action of this kind. All of us need a certain amount of natural light, and some seem to need more than others. Exposure to bright daylight can help lift your mood and leave you feeling good. Avoid spending too long in the dark during the day, as this may result in you feeling down. Take a walk in the park, visit the countryside, go to the coast, play golf, or simply stop for a drink at a pavement cafe.

Communication

It is by our behaviour that we are known. None of us has full and direct access to the internal experience of another. We can only infer that experience from what they say and do.

This presents us with two challenges. The first is that of sending the right messages. What can we do to help ensure that through our words and actions we accurately and effectively communicate with others? The second is that of getting the right message. What can we do to help ensure that we correctly interpret what others are communicating with us through their words or actions? The ability to do both these things well is a characteristic of psychological fitness.

Communication is the art of sending and receiving messages. What are the keys to doing this most effectively? I believe they can be summed up in three words: attitude, attention, and attachment.

Attitude

Communication starts in the heart. It is an inner event which may then be followed by outer expression. Words and actions are among the media by which we communicate; they are the channels, not the source.

The roots of communication lie within us, and it is from these that we draw whenever we open our mouth to speak. All that we are within combines to influence all that we say and do. Because of this, any work we do to constructively develop our inner world will have a beneficial impact on our communication.

We use the term attitude to describe the internal positions we adopt in relation to all that we experience. As we have seen, attitudes predispose us to feel, think, and act, in certain ways. Directly or indirectly, our communication reflects our attitudes.

Consider, for example, the possible impact on communication of a resentful attitude. The person, who is jealous of someone they see as having something they want, will tend to feel resentful whenever they see or think of the other. They will also tend to think resentfully, perhaps dwelling on how unfair or unfortunate it is that the other has been advantaged rather than them. Finally, their actions will reflect their jealousy. Perhaps they will rob the other of that which they desire, in order to possess it themselves, or simply work to ensure that the other person loses their privileged position.

On occasions I have heard resentful people putting into words their intentions to act in this way. Alternatively, they may seek to disguise their motives, not wanting their true attitude to be seen. But however carefully they choose their words to hide their heart other channels of communication may give them away to anyone with ears to hear it, or eyes to see it.

Were messages conveyed merely by the content of our words, such deception would be harder to spot, but because of the influential roles played by our tone of voice and body language, it is often possible to pick up the fact that 'something isn't quite right'. Closer observation may reveal discrepancies between words, tone of voice, and body language. For example, the words may express delight at the success of another, but the tone is tinged with jealousy, and accompanied by more of a frown than a smile!

Of course, we must be careful not to assume that such discrepancies necessarily indicate deception. Often the information communicated by each channel is different but congruent. In this case, the message conveyed by one channel does not contradict that conveyed by another. The words chosen by the person express only part of the message, additional information being conveyed through intonation and body language.

Clearly, we should seek to deal with any negative or unhelpful attitudes that might corrupt the messages we send, and distort our interpretation of the messages we receive. In addition it is helpful to cultivate constructive attitudes. There are many such attitudes that contribute powerfully to improved communication. Integrity, generosity, honesty, forgiveness, helpfulness, positivity, tactfulness, mercy, and, above all, compassion, are examples of attitudes that can transform not only communications, but also the relationships in which they are set.

When you talk to others practice identifying your own attitudes. See if you can find words or phrases that describe them. Whenever you identify an unhelpful attitude, reject it instantly, and deal with any underlying issues that may be helping to generate an attitude of this kind. Choose in its place a constructive attitude, and watch how things begin to change as you communicate from this new position.

Attention

If attitude has to do with knowing yourself, attention has to do with knowing your audience. Who are you seeking to communicate with? How well do you know this person, or this group of people? The more you know about the person or the people you are talking to, the better placed you will be to present your message in the most effective way.

Attention not only helps us understand the messages that other people send, but also to develop an understanding of the people themselves. Both are central to effective communication.

To attend is to focus on something, with awareness of the information it provides to any or all of our senses. It may include listening carefully to what others are saying – not just the content of their words, but also their tone of voice. It may also include observation, looking carefully (but not staring) at the other person, noting their facial expression, appearance, gestures, and other actions. In some circumstances there may be information from other senses also, such as the feel of a warm handshake, or the scent of a beautiful fragrance. All these say something about the person.

Wherever possible we should seek to give the other person our full attention. This is not always appropriate. For example, we may be engaged, individually or with others, in a complex or difficult task that itself requires our focused attention. But where it is possible, as in the majority of one-to-one conversations, giving your undivided attention will not only provide you with helpful information about the other, but also send a powerful message that you are interested in them and in what they have to say.

Attachment

Attitudes and attention only make their full impact when combined with a third characteristic of effective communication: attachment.

Attachment is the formation of a psychological connection by which information may be more freely exchanged between people. It may be compared to the making of an electrical connection. A connection must be established before electricity can be transmitted. If the wire is not properly attached, you have a loose connection, and you will not be able to rely on a consistent transmission of power. Power supply will likely be intermittent and unreliable. Communication is similar. The better your connection with the other person, the more likely it is that they will pay attention to you and hear what you have to say. The weaker your connection, the more likely it is that you may be neither seen nor heard.

To be an effective communicator, you must connect with those you would communicate with. Attachments enable the power of one mind to energise another. The transmission of ideas, no less than the transmission of an electrical impulse, relies upon a good connection being made.

How do you establish a connection of this kind? There are many things that may contribute to attachment, in the sense that we are using the word. One of the first is the way in which we approach other people. Moving towards others in a friendly and positive way is often a good start. It doesn't take most people long to pick up whether you are interested in them or not. Take a sincere interest in others, and in most cases they will respond positively to you. Ask about them, and listen with interest to their replies. If they share with you their successes, let them see how pleased you are for them. If they share with you their challenges or troubles, empathise with them, and don't be afraid to express your sympathy with emotional expressions such as sighs and mmm's, as well as in words.

When seeking to connect with another person, avoid the temptation to change the subject to something you would rather talk about, or are more comfortable with, but let them tell you what they want to say, whilst you listen with sincere expressions of interest, sympathy, or whatever is an appropriate response. Try to imagine what it might be like to be in their position.

You don't have to agree with the other person in order to connect with them, but in many cases you do have to talk their language. This is not just a matter of you both speaking in the same tongue, but extends to using similar intonation and body language, as appropriate.

If you can stay in this mode for a while, you will often reach a point where you sense that a connection has been made with the other person. Take the time to understand the person and their message. Listen carefully, and ask questions, in order to reach this point. If necessary, test out your understanding by asking the other person to tell you whether you've got it right or not. All this strengthens the connection between you.

On those occasions when you disagree with the position taken by the other person, you don't need to sacrifice your own views and opinions, but you do need to be able to see things from their point of view, however much it might differ from your own. As you communicate the fact that you understand, you will often find that others open up to you and that an attachment is formed.

Finally, it is always a good idea to think before you speak, and especially so when seeking to connect with another. Ask yourself "What is the best thing to say here and how is it best said?"

When it comes to sending messages, you have a lot of choice. This includes the decision of whether or not to speak, the choice of message to convey, the words you will use, your tone of voice, the volume of your voice, your facial expressions, your posture, the gestures you make, and the actions you take. All these should be congruent. Don't say one thing and do another. The less people feel they can trust you, the less open they are likely to be to your message. If you find yourself sending mixed messages, stop and sort out any personal issues of your own that are causing, or contributing to, that incongruence.

Occupation

People need to be engaged in some kind of meaningful activity. You need to feel that the work you do is worthwhile, and to be able to look back at the end of each working day and see that you have done something, or created something, of value.

To achieve this, you may need to make a distinction between your life's work and your paid employment. Your life's work is your unique contribution, the work you believe in, a purpose that moves you. Your paid work is just that – the work you are paid to do.

Your life's work and your paid work may be one and the same, entirely different, or overlapping to some degree. Whilst it might be ideal to be paid to do what you most believe in, this is not always possible in practice.

What is your life's work? You may or may not have given this question much thought before now. If you haven't, pause for a moment and consider what your response might be.

In order not to be restricted by self imposed limitations, you may find it helpful to ask, "If I could do absolutely anything during my time here on earth, what would it be?" Other helpful questions might include:

- What are my gifts and skills?
- What would I like to do?
- Is there something I feel I should devote my life to?
- How could I make a difference?
- What is the most worthwhile contribution I could make?
- What would I like written on my tombstone?

As you answer these questions, don't entertain any question of whether or not you can be paid for your life's work, at this stage. Earning from it may or may not be possible. Also, don't limit your thoughts to recognised occupational categories.

Your life's work may involve you in one or more recognised roles, but it may not. You have a unique role that no one else can take. It is this role that you must find and fill, if you are to experience the greatest job satisfaction and fulfilment.

Having reflected on these questions, write a few lines describing the picture so far, a short statement that expresses what you would like to do. Don't worry if it is vague or imprecise at this stage. You can develop the picture, making changes and adding detail, as you go on. Briefly describe your life's work, as you see it today.

Keep your description to hand, so that you can add further details and insights as they come to you. Even when the picture is pretty clear, and requires little or no further amendment, you will still find it helpful to keep this statement in a place where you will often see it. This will help you keep on track, doing the things that are most important to you. Given the many demands and pressures that life sends, it is easy to sacrifice the important for the urgent.

Whatever your employment situation, start today on your life's work. Ask yourself, "What can I do today? What do I have the power to do now?" There will be something you can do now that contributes to your great work or prepares you more fully for it.

Prioritise your life's work, keep firm control of it, and, as far as you are able, do not let anyone hijack it. You may not be the boss in your paid work, but you must always keep executive control over your life's work. You must remain true to your greatest purpose.

Living out that purpose can be challenging. However clear your view of your mission might be, the process of following it from day-to-day may be far from clear. Fulfilling your mission is an emergent process, unfolding as you move through it.

Progress tends to be one step at a time. You see a step, you take it, and then you see the next step.

Maximised mindpower requires our life's work, but financial necessity requires paid work. Whilst for some these may be one and the same, for others they may be quite different.

If your paid work is unfulfilling, you may be able to change it for something more meaningful, but if that is not possible, you still have the option of doing something worthwhile. Your wages may pay your bills, but your life's work will satisfy your soul. Your unpaid work may be the most important thing you do.

One person might develop their creative work as an artist, writer, or musician. Another might engage in charitable work, bringing comfort, support and relief to others. Yet another might raise psychologically healthy and well adjusted children. The possibilities for meaningful and worthwhile employment are many and varied.

Even if you are in the unfortunate position of not being able to obtain paid employment, you can still do worthwhile work. Your resources are likely to be more limited, perhaps desperately so, but however restricted or straightened your circumstances, no one can take the vision from your heart. Whilst you live, your mission remains. Do what you can to fulfil it, whatever happens.

Exploration

Exploration has to do with how we approach our world. Psychologically fit people are better able to engage appropriately with their environment. They move towards reality, exploring it, testing it, and working with it as best they can. In contrast, the less mentally fit people are, the more they tend to move away from reality, distorting it for their own convenience, and projecting on to it their own alternative version of the way things are.

What is it about reality that makes people want to run away from it? The short answer is anxiety. Whenever you feel threatened or anxious, you need to decide whether the threat you see is an actual or a potential problem.

This is a key distinction. If you can see that a threatening incident is actually taking place, you have two basic choices: fight or flight. For example, if you're anxious because you see a bus coming straight towards you, you need to get out of the way as quickly as you can! But if it is not actually happening, you need to do a risk assessment. How likely is it that the thing you fear will happen? What is the real level of threat? Ideally, you will correctly assess whether the risk is low, moderate, or high, and then take whatever action in appropriate.

Problems arise when our assessment of risk is incorrect. If you tell yourself that something bad is likely to happen, when it is unlikely, you will experience an inappropriately high level of anxiety. If you then persist in what you are doing, without correcting your assessment, you are likely to remain anxious, and find the experience more emotionally and physically draining than it needs to be.

But if you stop what you are doing and withdraw from the situation, pulling back from the perceived threat, you will likely experience immediate relief. The anxiety rapidly subsides as you retreat to a safe place. Because escape is so rewarding, in terms of the relief it brings, you may repeat this behaviour again and again, until it becomes an automatic and unconscious part of your day-to-day life. The result is a diminished existence.

By this means, things we would love to do are lost to us, opportunity after opportunity is missed, and our suffering, of which there is already enough in life, is significantly increased.

Overestimating risk is, of course, only one of the two possible risk assessment errors that we may make. Underestimating or denying risk, is the opposite problem. If you tell yourself that something bad is unlikely to happen to you, when it is likely, you will experience an inappropriately low level of anxiety, or even a complete absence of anxiety (if you have taken the incorrect view that there is no threat at all). Should you continue in this mode, you are in real danger, as your capacity to assess risk and respond appropriately to it has been compromised.

Incorrect assessments of risk often lead to problems. No one is perfect at risk assessment. We all get it wrong sometimes. By honestly appraising your own assessments of risk, you can recognise when you get it wrong, and then seek to deal with your issues, the personal biases that are distorting your perceptions of danger and limiting your exploration of your world.

What does this involve? Firstly, correctly assess the risk. Whatever your level of anxiety, be honest about the actual level of risk. Seek to take an objective look at the situation, and ask yourself whether the level of risk is low, high, or somewhere in between. Whenever you face or think about this situation, consciously and deliberately tell yourself the truth about the actual level of risk. For example, if you have been telling yourself that it is likely your plane will crash, start saying that it is unlikely, and say it every time you think of a plane, see a plane, or fly on a plane.

Secondly, stand your ground, do that thing, and do not give in to your fear. Your fear is a false alarm, telling you it is dangerous when it isn't. You cannot just turn that alarm off, but you can override it. Feel the fear, but do it anyway. Keep doing the thing you fear, all the while telling yourself the truth about the likelihood of danger, and you will gradually reprogram your mind to respond differently in the future.

By training your mind to make more correct assessments of risk, you may overcome the widespread human tendency to inappropriate withdrawal, and thereby avoid the loss that such withdrawal brings. Renewed confidence will enable you to explore your world again, moving towards life and others, rather than away from them. Exploration facilitates discovery, and discovery facilitates development. Without the confidence and courage to explore, it is unlikely that you will ever discover who you truly are, or make the most of either your mind or your life.

10
People Need People

Managing relationships

Our psychological fitness is linked to our relationships and the way we manage them. All of us need a certain quantity and quality of social interaction if we are going to enjoy a good level of mind health. In this chapter we will be looking at some of the keys to managing relationships effectively.

Find those who are good for you

People need people. The beneficial influence on mental health of a supportive social context has long been recognised.

Everyone needs social contact, although the amount required differs somewhat from one person to another. Those who are more extraverted seem to need more contact with others, whilst the more introverted appear to need less. How much do you think you need to function at your best? Take a look at your current level of social interaction. Is it enough, too much, or too little?

If it is too much, what could you do to get the space you need? If it is too little, what could you do to increase it? Whatever your personality, don't spend too long on your own. Get out and meet people. Consider joining local groups or clubs that are of interest to you, or volunteer to help with charities or other organisations that rely heavily on voluntary support.

It is not just the quantity of social contact that's important for psychological fitness, but the quality of social interaction. We all need to connect positively with others. Keep in touch with loved ones and friends. It doesn't take long to make a call, to send an email, or to send a text message, but it can have a big impact on how you feel.

People influence each other in different ways. Think about the people you know and the effect they each have on your state of mind. You will probably detect some differences.

For optimum health of mind we need an appropriate balance between those whose company is better for us, and those whose company is less good for us. Try to ensure that, amongst those who are closest to you, there are some who influence you in a positive way. If necessary, look for additional people who are good for you, to add to your friends.

When it comes to identifying those who are good for you, look for positive qualities. For example, is the person fun to be with? Are they easy to get along with? Do they like you? Are they positive and upbeat? Do they let you be yourself? Do you feel energised in their company? Do they have a sense of humour? Do they want the best for you?

Find those who are good for you, and spend time with them, but remember that you are unlikely to find anyone who has all the qualities you like. Don't make the mistake of looking for perfect people. They don't exist.

At first glance, some people might look as though they would be good for you, but in reality they are not. In this respect, try not to select those who always agree with you, or those who encourage your dysfunctional attitudes or actions (such as avoiding situations you find challenging, but which you know you need to face). Those who will have the best influence on you will include people who love you enough to challenge you, or to tell you when they think you might be making a mistake.

Just as some people are good for us, there may be others who are not so good for us. Those whose company always leaves us feeling exhausted, anxious, angry, guilty, a failure, hopeless, or depressed, are amongst those with whom we should probably have restricted contact. The same might be said of those who make excessive or inappropriate use of manipulation, intimidation, or domination, in order to control others and get what they want.

If you have too much contact with negative, controlling, or particularly dysfunctional people, it may adversely influence your mood, or state of mind.

Try to ensure, as far as you can, that you spend enough time with the people who build you up, and not too much time with those who pull you down. It's not about spending all your time with the positive people, and avoiding the negative ones. It's about getting the right balance. This is a personal challenge. Only you can decide on the mix that is best for you.

Amongst those who are a positive influence in your life, it can be good to have one or more people with whom you can share more deeply or fully. Being able to discuss problems and difficulties, or challenges and opportunities, with others can sometimes help us to see things more clearly, get a better perspective, and base our decisions on a wider pool of knowledge and wisdom.

Some people are more helpful than others in this respect. Those who are informed, wise, and trustworthy, are often amongst the best. Before entrusting someone else with sensitive personal information, check out their ability to handle and to be trusted with your personal data. Everyone's different. One person may be good with issues of a particular kind, whilst another may be good at handling issues of a different kind. One person may be exceptionally trustworthy, with whom many aspects of your private world may be safely shared, whilst another may have no commitment to confidentiality, making them a highly unsuitable counsellor or confidante. Take the time to get to know people. Find out who you can share with, and what you can confidently share with them.

Asking for help

However knowledgeable, gifted, or competent we may be, none of us knows everything or possesses every skill. There will be times when we need the help of others to achieve our goals. At such times, the people who are good for us are those who can help us in some way. Psychologically fit people ask for help when they need it. They recognise that asking for help at such times is a sign of strength rather than weakness, a sign of good management rather than incompetence.

Some of those whose minds are not so fit struggle to do this. One person may be afraid to ask for help, thinking that they may look stupid or incompetent, if they do. Another may be too proud to ask, seeing such a request as an admission of weakness that may cost them the respect of others. Yet another may have such a deep distrust of others that they are unwilling to risk the bad treatment they believe they might receive, should they make themselves vulnerable in this way. Whatever the reason, if you find it hard to ask for help when you need it, be honest with yourself about why this is, and then get to work on correcting any unhelpful attitudes or habits.

There may be times when the kind of help we need is directly related to our psychological fitness. Perhaps we want to develop specific personal skills, such as improving our time management, and a coach helps us to become better players in the game of life. Perhaps we face personal issues that we struggle to resolve, such as dealing with anger, and a counsellor helps us make the journey to better functioning. Perhaps we suffer from depression, or some form of mental illness, and a medical doctor or psychiatrist gives us treatment to control or heal our infirmity.

Don't be afraid to seek help for your mind, if good professional help is available and you need it.

Forgive those who wrong you

Given the darker side of human nature, it is inevitable that all of us will be wronged by others. Even where no wrong exists or is intended, our capacity to imagine, as well as our tendency to misinterpret the intentions and actions of others combine to ensure that we will feel wronged.

Unresolved, the emotions generated by perceived wrongs can undermine our psychological health, poisoning the mind and rendering it unable to operate at its best. Unless and until their venom is neutralised, these painful feelings and their associated thoughts can bias our perceptions, distort our thinking, limit our actions, and rob us of happiness.

The best word I know to describe the healing process for the pain of being wronged is forgiveness. Forgiveness is overcoming your negative thoughts and feelings neither by denying the wrong, nor your right to be angry or hurt, but by cancelling the debt owed you by another. You see the offender as one who, like yourself, stands in need of forgiveness, and you release them from their debt, reducing your personal expectations of them to the level of their current performance, so that you can be healed.

Note that forgiveness is not condoning the wrongs done to you. It's rejecting rather than accepting them. Forgiveness is letting them go. Why hold on to something that is only going to do you harm? If an animal bit you, the last thing you would do would be to grab the creature and hold it so close that it couldn't let go of your body! No, you would do everything in your power to get away. Forgiveness is breaking free.

It starts with a simple decision to forgive, whether or not we feel like forgiving, and it is followed by a process in which we are progressively released from the toxic effects of our pain.

Stop now for a moment to consider the wrongs you have experienced at the hands of others. Starting with the most serious, and taking them one at a time, I suggest you face honestly how you feel, and call to mind the person, or people, involved.

As you recall each one in the privacy of your own mind, tell them you forgive them, and reset your expectations to the level they acted at. You can hope that people will improve their ways, and in some cases you may be able to help them change, but you cannot afford to live under the illusion that they are better than they are. Facing the facts of where they are at, destroys that illusion, and will help you get free from the pain of their wrong.

Don't let anger and bitterness towards others corrupt your mind and hijack your life. Adopt forgiveness as an integral part of your daily lifestyle. Forgive quickly, forgive freely, forgive fully, and forgive all.

Help those you can

It's tough when you are in trouble, and those who have the power to help you don't. But when the roles are reversed and you have the power to help others, do you? The willingness to give help and to receive it, are both characteristics of a fit mind.

If you want to *feel* good, *do* good. Help someone out, smile, get involved and make a contribution, perform a random act of kindness, give something away, or rescue somebody.

If you know someone who is feeling down, or struggling in some way, why not give them a call, or meet them for a tea or coffee? Don't wait for them to contact you. When people are feeling low, they often find it hard to approach others. Your calls and ongoing support may make all the difference. Just knowing that you care and that you are standing with them may be a great help.

When you are with other people, get into the habit of looking for needs you can help meet. If you are not sure how to help a person, ask them, "How can I help you? What would you find helpful?"

Be careful not to fall into the trap of seeing value and giving solely in financial or material terms. A person with little money and few possessions still has the greatest things to give. Love, hope, and faith cannot be bought with any amount of money.

Some of the greatest gifts are non-material in nature. Give a thirsty person a bottle of water and you quench their thirst once, but give them the knowledge to dig a well, and you give them a continual water supply. The knowledge contained in these pages is of this kind. It has the power to transform minds and lives. Consider giving someone a copy of this book. It may be one of the single most helpful things you do for them.

11
Strategies for Living

People as strategists

If I seek achievement so that people will admire or respect me, or wealth so that I can buy whatever I desire, or if I stay away from other people in order to avoid the possibility of being rejected, I am pursuing a strategy that is designed to make me feel better.

People are strategists. They naturally make plans. The capacity to assess your situation and respond in the way you believe is most likely to achieve your purpose, is something you were born with.

A strategy is a plan for achieving a specific objective. When you decide on how best to build a friendship, how best to manage your finances, or how best to use your time, you are strategising. Whether we are aware of it or not, each of us makes plans as part of our management of life. We are all strategic planners.

Many strategies, like those just mentioned, relate to particular situations or areas of life. Influential though these may be, their impact upon us is less pervasive than the strategies we adopt to achieve our life objectives. We call these life strategies.

A life strategy is a plan for living. It is one of the ways in which you have chosen to manage your life, and to respond to its challenges. Life presents us with both opportunities and threats, each of which requires a strategic response. For example, how are we going to get our needs met? What can we do to enjoy life more? How can we diminish the psychological pain of rejection? How are we going to be who we really are? How are we going to fulfil the goals in life that are important to us?

The way you have learnt to respond to life situations, combined with your answers to these and other life questions, will create your personal life strategies.

Let's take a look at them.

Check out your strategies

There are various ways of exploring life strategies. One is to work on your own, examining your own experience and behaviour in order to identify your strategies.

Alternatively, you could explore them with someone else who's knowledgeable in this area. This might be in the context of coaching, counselling, psychotherapy, or some other personal development setting.

Another possibility is to complete the Life Strategy Indicator (LSI), a psychological measure I developed to help people quickly and reliably identify their strategies. As a professionally researched and properly validated indicator, the LSI is the best way I know to get an accurate overview of your strategic world. Experienced therapists might identify major strategies to some degree, but not necessarily to build as full and accurate picture as that provided by the LSI, which gives a full profile of the person in terms of 35 major strategies. The value of such data for personal development is great indeed.

There isn't the space in this chapter to include the full LSI, but what we can do is to ask some of the questions that are often helpful in highlighting strategies, and then use this information to identify which of the 35 strategies we rely upon most.

On the following pages you will find a simple exercise of this kind. In the first table you will find a list of questions, with a space opposite each one in which to write your one word answers.

As you answer the questions, try to do so as honestly as you can, and without censoring your initial responses. Sometimes our first thoughts are very revealing and point to strategies we may be wholly or partly unconscious of, but which we need to be fully aware of if we are going to develop healthy strategies for living. If you get stuck on a question, move on to the next one, and come back to it at the end.

Some Life Questions	*Your One Word Answers*
What would you say was the most important thing in your life?	
What other things are important to you?	
What would you say is the best way to make the most of your life?	
What other things are important when it comes to making the most of life?	
How do you typically cope with threats?	
How do you typically respond to opportunities?	
How would you describe your approach to life?	
What do you do to make your life enjoyable?	
What do you do to make your life successful?	
What do you do to feel good about yourself?	
What do you do to make your life less emotionally painful?	
What have you found to be the most important attitude to adopt in life?	
What other attitudes do you think are particularly helpful?	

When you have finished answering the questions, turn to the next tables which contain 35 of the most common strategies, with a brief description of each one. Then take each of your answer words in turn, and match it to the strategy it most closely relates to. There is a space next to each strategy where you can write the matching word from the first table.

For example, if you wrote that work was one of the most important things to you, and that you believe that an attitude of hard work contributes to success in life, then you have identified a *Work* strategy.

When you have finished, you will have classified your answers in terms of the life strategies they reflect. You may find it helpful to underline or highlight the strategies you have identified.

Life Strategies	
Strategy	*Matching Words*
1 **Self Knowledge**: *Life is best lived from a position of knowing oneself*	
2 **Self Esteem**: *Life is best lived from the position of a good self relationship*	
3 **Self Reliance**: *Life is best lived from a position of independence and autonomy*	
4 **Self Control**: *Life is best lived with self discipline and self restraint*	
5 **Anti Self**: *Life is best lived with a negative view of oneself*	
6 **Health**: *Life is best lived from a position of physical health and fitness*	
7 **Spirituality**: *Life is best lived in personal relationship with God*	
8 **Social Acceptance**: *Life is best lived in relationship with others*	
9 **Helping**: *Life is best lived from a position of giving to others*	
10 **Commitment**: *Life is best lived with loyalty, dependability and responsibility*	
11 **Recognition**: *Life is best lived from a position of being admired and respected*	
12 **Life Partnership**: *Life is best lived in close relationship with a life partner*	

| Life Strategies ||
Strategy	Matching Words
13 **Parenting**: *Life is best lived from a position of raising children*	
14 **Modelling**: *Life is best lived by copying or imitating someone you admire*	
15 **Helplessness**: *Life is best lived if others look after you*	
16 **Social Control**: *Life is best lived by influencing or manipulating others*	
17 **Anti Social**: *Life is best lived from an aggressive position towards others*	
18 **Appearance**: *Life is best lived by being seen in a certain way*	
19 **Purpose**: *Life is best lived by pursuing ones vision and purpose*	
20 **Knowledge**: *Life is best lived in the pursuit of learning*	
21 **Wisdom**: *Life is best lived by making wise choices and decisions*	
22 **Honesty**: *Life is best lived from a position of openness, integrity and truthfulness*	
23 **Positivity**: *Life is best lived with a positive outlook on life*	
24 **Courage**: *Life is best lived with daring and bravery*	

Life Strategies	
Strategy	*Matching Words*
25 **Enjoyment**: Life is best lived in the pursuit of happiness and pleasure	
26 **Life Acceptance**: Life is best lived from a position of resigned acceptance	
27 **Change**: Life is best lived by changing things and making a difference	
28 **Creativity**: Life is best lived by expressing creative ability	
29 **Competence**: Life is best lived by doing things well	
30 **Work**: Life is best lived by hard work and achievement	
31 **Acquisition**: Life is best lived by material, financial, or other gain	
32 **Perseverance**: Life is best lived from a position of patience, persistence and determination	
33 **Survival**: Life is best lived by finding a way of getting through its difficulties and trials	
34 **Selective Awareness**: Life is best lived by selectively focusing on certain things	
35 **Avoidance**: Life is best lived by withdrawing from things one finds unpleasant or threatening	

How effective are your strategies?

A good strategy is one which not only achieves its purpose but also contributes to psychological fitness and health. If I adopt a strategy of *Avoidance* it may be very effective in reducing my anxiety, but it may also severely limit my effectiveness in key areas, such as my relationships and my work.

Some strategies help to optimise our experience and achievement, increasing our psychological well being. Others have the opposite effect, undermining our enjoyment of life and compromising our mental fitness.

How would you rate your own strategies? I'd like you to turn back to the strategy table and ask yourself two simple questions in relation to each strategy you identified. Firstly: does it work? How effective is it in achieving its objectives? Secondly: does it increase your psychological fitness and well being?

As you evaluate your strategies, try to be radically honest with yourself. Remember that there is no advantage in pretending that something is working better than it actually is.

Bear in mind that some strategies are essentially unhelpful and represent inherently dysfunctional approaches to managing life. These include the *Anti Self*, *Helplessness*, and *Anti Social* strategies. If you find that you are using a strategy of this kind, don't panic! It is far better to know, than to remain unaware. Knowledge is power. Once you have identified a toxic strategy, you are in a position to take remedial action.

Other strategies, such as *Social Control, Selective Awareness*, and *Avoidance*, may also represent dysfunction, depending on the way in which the strategy is used. If you are using a *Social Control* strategy, ask yourself whether the power you seek to exercise is legitimate, or based on the use of manipulation, intimidation or domination. If you recognise that you are making significant use of *Selective Awareness* as a life strategy, ask yourself whether you are screening data on the basis of what you need to know, or as a way of avoiding seeing things you find threatening. If *Avoidance* is one of your major strategies, ask yourself whether you are avoiding real threats, or whether you are running away from things you should be facing.

Changing strategies

Whenever we identify and evaluate a strategy, it puts us in a position to make changes, should we wish to. We are unlikely to want to change strategies that are effective and contribute to a fit mind, but less effective or dysfunctional strategies are another matter.

What changes would you like to make to your own strategies? Take each of them in turn and ask this question. You may wish to change the way you use a strategy, scrap the strategy altogether, or develop a new strategy. Let's look at each of these options.

Often we can improve on the way we use a strategy. Most of the 35 major strategies listed here are not inherently unhelpful or unhealthy, but we may be using them in a less than helpful, unhelpful, or unhealthy way that undermines our mental fitness, well being, and mindpower.

For example, one person's *Social Acceptance* strategy might represent a healthy appreciation of social interaction, but another's might reflect an obsessive demand that they be accepted by everyone. Because of this, it is important to be honest with yourself about what each of your strategies means for you. If you recognise that you are using a strategy in a less than helpful, unhelpful, or unhealthy way, ask yourself what a healthy expression of the strategy might look like. Then write a short sentence that captures this, read it every morning, and practice doing it each day until you do it automatically and without thinking.

As we have seen, there are some strategies that are essentially dysfunctional. For example, an *Anti-Social* strategy will generate relational and other problems, isolating the strategist from others and making healthy relationships impossible. If you find that you are using a dysfunctional strategy, write a one sentence statement expressing your rejection of it as a way of managing your life, read your statement every morning, and put it into practice each day, until you find that you are no longer using this unhealthy means of life management.

You may decide that you need a new strategy. For example, someone may feel that they are not using their creativity, and decide to adopt *Creativity* as a strategy for enriching their leisure and for increasing their enjoyment of life. You can build a new strategy at any time, but you will need to give yourself a few months to get it established. If you feel that this is something you need to do, write a sentence or two describing what it might look like in practice for you to use the new strategy. Read your statement every morning, and keep putting it into practice until it becomes an established part of your life, something you do automatically and without thinking.

Build the strategies that enable you to make the most of your mind and your life.

12
Bouncing Back

How resilient are you?

Everyone knows that a flat ball is a dead ball. If there's no air in the ball, it won't bounce, but pump it up and it'll bounce back. It's not just balls that lose their bounce. People do too.

What happens to you when you trip up, or you are pushed over, as you make your way along the road of life? Do you determine to get back on your feet, whatever it takes, or do you give up?

This chapter is about how to bounce back, or to use the psychological term, developing resilience. Resilience is drawing on both inner and outer resources in order to cope well with adversity. Resilient people are better able to persevere in the face of difficulty and to bounce back from defeat and failure. They are flexible in adapting to change, and willing to learn new things.

However fit your mind may be you will still have to face the challenges and trials of life. Bad things happen to fit and unfit alike. The difference is that the fitter you are psychologically, the better you will be able to cope when tough times come. Everyone experiences challenge and change, but not everyone has developed the resilience to cope well with such events.

Resilience helps us deal with the losses, disappointments, and crises of life. We will still face stress, as well as unpleasant emotions such as anxiety, anger, or sadness, but we will do so better equipped to cope with adversity.

Resilience training

Some people seem to be born with more resilient personalities. From an early age they appear to cope better with frustration and stress than others do. But although there may be a genetic component to resilience, it is far from being the whole story. People can learn to be resilient.

Consider the emergency services professional by way of example. He or she has been rigorously trained to respond to particular kinds of crisis in a highly disciplined and resilient way. Faced with a building on fire, a crime taking place, or an accident involving seriously injured people, this person keeps a clear head, stays focused, and does the job they have been trained to do.

You don't have to join the emergency services to become resilient, but whoever you are, you can learn resilience, and by so doing dramatically increase your ability to cope with whatever life throws at you. Having trained yourself in the necessary skills, to the level where they become your automatic responses, you will find that you can increasingly rely on yourself to respond helpfully in difficult situations.

What are these skills? In the next few pages we will be looking at how to build resilience. As we do, you will notice that although the resilient often make effective use of outer resources, it is on inner foundations that resilience is established.

Be your own buddy

Resilience starts with the self. How you relate to yourself will have a major impact on your resilience level.

Just as the effectiveness of a military unit depends upon the commitment of its soldiers to fight, and if necessary die for each other, so the effectiveness of the individual depends on the quality of the self relationship. If the self relationship is good, there will be a foundation on which resilience may be built, but anything less than being your own buddy will undermine your ability to fight in the battle of life. Being divided in yourself, your resilience will be compromised.

Whatever your faults and failings, you must befriend yourself and believe that your life and your mission are worth fighting for. Only then can those faults be defeated, and life's victory won.

See yourself as resilient

How do you see yourself? Do you think of yourself as being more of a 'can do' person, or do you feel that you are more of a 'can't do' person? Your answer will reflect your resilience level.

Like the self relationship, the self concept is an important contributor to resilience. See yourself as a survivor. If you don't see yourself as coping well, it is unlikely that you will. In fact, if you see yourself as a loser, you have probably lost already.

Develop a survivor mentality. At the heart of resilience is a decision to believe that somehow you are going to make it through. Tell yourself that you will get through, one way or another, but don't indulge in unrealistic expectations in order to pep yourself up, such as, "It'll be OK in a week's/month's/year's time." If you do, when that time comes, and it is still not OK, you will likely be disappointed, disillusioned, and depressed. Instead, take it one day at a time.

Confront your challenges

Faced with a problem, you have two basic options: fight or flight. Some people fight everything in sight, whilst others flee even when no one is chasing them! Neither is resilient.

Resilient people confront the challenges they need to address. This is not the same thing as deliberately courting danger or picking fights, but a deliberate policy of dealing with the issues that need to be faced, rather than ignoring them in the hope that they'll go away of their own accord.

How you see challenges and difficulties will help to determine your attitude in this respect. If you see them as insurmountable, you will likely run from them. But if you recognise that opportunity comes with every trouble and trial, you will find the courage to proceed.

Without denying real dangers, determine to see every crisis as an opportunity to learn, to grow, and to better fulfil your purpose in life, despite the fact that how this is to be achieved will often be hidden from view. Remember that without challenge and difficulty there is no progress. Anything of value comes at a price.

Face reality and make a constructive response

In any battle, including the battle of life, it is helpful to know your enemy. What exactly are you facing? Try to make an objective assessment of the problem. You may find it helpful to write things down. Expressing your difficulties on paper can bring clarity and help you get things in better perspective.

In your response to problems you need to avoid the equal and opposite dangers of denying the negative aspects of the situation and dwelling morbidly on them. Denial sometimes masquerades as resilience, but it is only a hollow counterfeit. People may refuse to face the unpleasant aspects of a situation as a way of coping, but this invariably results in them coping less well. Having censored important data, they fail to take this information into account in their decision making, with potentially damaging (or even disastrous) consequences for themselves and others. Feeding negatively on the problem is no better. It solves nothing, increases the likelihood of depression and despair, and makes it less likely that constructive responses will be seen.

Resilient people face the facts, including the 'bad' news, but seek to make a constructive response informed by the information available to them at the time. They neither deny reality, nor dwell unhelpfully upon it.

Practice under pressure

The poet Rudyard Kipling wrote, "If you can keep your head when all about you are losing theirs and blaming it on you; if you can trust yourself when all men doubt you, but make allowance for their doubting too..." What are you like under pressure?

Resilient people are better able in the midst of a crisis to remain focused on the task at hand. Like the pilot who does everything possible to land the plane safely when the engines have failed, the resilient person has learnt to sufficiently suppress fear and anxiety so that he or she can attend fully to the task for as long as required.

The best way to learn how to cope well in a crisis is to practice dealing with crisis situations. Try to see every challenge you face as an opportunity to develop your skills in this area, and so become a more resilient person.

Be flexible

Trees don't generally snap, and we know why. It's because they bend. Bend or break – that's the choice! You cannot stop the wind blowing, but you can move with the wind. Resilience is flexibility.

Faced with the challenge of change, inflexible people struggle to adapt, and should they fail to do so, loss is the usual outcome. But those who choose to be flexible adjust better to the changing needs of the situation. They draw from the helpful lessons they have learnt in the past, but they are also ready to learn new ways of seeing and doing things, and may even come up with creative solutions to the crises they face.

Flexibility does not require that you compromise your principles or core values, but that you apply them in a way that is appropriate to the present situation. Life is complex, and there are often many different factors influencing every situation. Take the time to find out the facts, as best you can, and then, like a tree, bend with the wind.

Master your emotions

Another poet, William Blake once said, "If you're in a passion, much good may you do, but not much good if a passion is in you." Passion is vital to your psychological health, but only as your servant, never your master.

Resilient people have discovered how to avoid being derailed by toxic emotions when facing stress and trauma. They do this by acknowledging strong feelings and managing them effectively, expressing feelings where appropriate and suppressing powerful emotions where necessary, in order to stay as calm as possible, keep a clear head, and take constructive action. By so doing, they avoid being unduly influenced or overwhelmed by painful emotions during the crisis. After the crisis has passed, suppressed feelings can be brought to the surface and dealt with.

Call for help

If you're in trouble and you call for help, there's often more chance of being rescued than if you keep silent. Requesting assistance when it is needed is something resilient people do. In fact, some are particularly adept at eliciting support from those around them.

Although its roots are internal, and its fruits are often expressed in autonomous action, resilience is enhanced by the presence of a support network made up of those upon whom the person can rely for assistance when needed. Take a look at your own social network, and identify those who give you support and encouragement. These are the people to call on when you need help. If you cannot identify anyone like this, you are in a vulnerable position.

Have faith

Throughout history, many have found the greatest resilience by drawing not merely on personal skill and interpersonal support, but on the strength and comfort provided by a living faith.

Put your trust in the Highest Power, who knows suffering and loves you, to strengthen you, guide you, and ultimately deliver you from all harm.

13
To Infinity!

Beyond yourself

Up to this point we have been building mindpower with personal and interpersonal resources. Our aim has been to take the resources within each one of us, and apply them effectively to increase psychological health and fitness. But what happens when the executive power of the soul and the beneficial influences of others have been harnessed, and yet the soul is not fully satisfied? What do we do when we have come as far as we can within the limitations of human nature, but we desire still greater mindpower?

You don't have to look further than yourself to see those limitations. They include your experience, your knowledge, your wisdom, your intelligence, your health, your physical ability, your material and financial wealth, your contacts, your influence, your power, your time, your life span, your energy, your memory, your skills, and your creativity.

If we want more, we must find a way of transcending these limitations, a way of drawing from resources beyond our own. We need to connect with the power of a greater mind.

Have you ever wondered whether there is a Creator? If you have, it's an intelligent question. If I showed you a house, a car, or a machine for washing dishes, you wouldn't marvel at how such constructions came about all by themselves, or at how they evolved to their present state without human assistance! Faced with the overwhelming evidence of intelligent design, only one conclusion is reasonable: there is a designer. Say that your washing machine put itself together, or was the marvellous fruit of elements randomly colliding, and others may question your psychological health.

There is no greater mind than that of Infinite Intelligence. To be joined with the Mind that moves the planets and the stars is the apex of mindpower.

But how do we become compatible with the Eternal? Who will change our nature so that we can connect and communicate with the most powerful Mind of all? Thankfully the Creator, who alone has power to effect such a change, chose to become human, so that we might become divine.

To experience this fundamental change of nature and connect with God, all you need to do is ask Him for it. Pray this prayer:

> *Lord Jesus Christ, please change my nature and bring me into a living relationship with you. You took my sins upon yourself when you died on the cross in my place, paying the penalty I deserved, that I might go free. Thank you for your sacrifice. I confess my sins to you, particularly those upon my conscience (confess any specific wrongs to God) and I ask your forgiveness. I receive your gift of everlasting life, and I give my life wholly to you. From this day on, I will trust you fully, and follow you with my whole heart. Fill me now with your Holy Spirit and guide me always in your perfect will for my life. Amen.*

Meeting your deepest need

One of the most fundamental limitations we face is the inability to satisfy our deepest need. There is a deep hunger in every soul that cries out to be met. Until it is satisfied it gives the mind no rest. Day and night it demands attention, so that the mind is never free from the challenge of trying to satisfy it or silence it, neither of which it can achieve.

Are you aware that there is a hunger within you that physical food can never satisfy, that relationships can never satisfy, that money and possessions can never satisfy? This is a thirst you are unable to quench alone, a hunger that you are unable to assuage. Your spirit will never be satisfied by physical or psychological food, however rich you may be in these things. Spiritual food alone will satisfy your spiritual hunger. Just as the body feeds on meat or vegetables, and the mind feeds on ideas, so the spirit feeds on spirit.

But how do you feed the spirit? Thankfully, the answer is easy, so easy that even young children can do it. You turn to the Source of spirit. You make God your best friend.

God is Spirit. Listen to Him, and as you do His Spirit will feed your spirit. Any complex design works best when its maker's instructions are followed. As a created being, designed by God, you will only make the most of your mind and maximise its power when you listen to Him. You need to talk to the One who made you.

This is an inner activity. You listen to God within yourself, in the same way that you listen to your own inner voice.

It's a bit like imagining the voice of someone speaking to you. Think of someone you know of, but don't know personally. It could be anyone you like. Now imagine meeting them and talking together. What can you imagine that person saying to you?

Of course, the analogy of listening to an imagined human voice is limited in value, simply because it *is* an imagined voice. We know that the person is not actually saying those words. We have imagined it. If it were possible for us to connect our mind with theirs, so that we could actually hear them speaking to us, but without any physical means of transmission, it would be a different story.

The difference between imagining the voice of another person and listening to God is that God is really there. Unlike humans, He is everywhere, an omnipresent spirit.

Whereas human communication requires either the physical presence of the other, or a physical means of communication, such as a telephone, communication with God is different. Because He is everywhere, you can listen to Him anywhere and at any time. Wherever you are, He is there too. Wherever you go, He is already there. He is with you now, as you read this, and if you stop and listen, He will speak to you. That word will feed your spirit, meeting the deepest need of your soul.

If you have not already developed this skill, I invite you to start now. If possible, find a quiet place where you are not likely to be disturbed. With practice, you will find yourself increasingly able to hear God in busy or noisy places, but at the start it can be helpful to find a quiet spot, free from distractions.

Next, relax your body and quieten your mind, laying your thoughts and concerns aside. You may find when you do this that all kinds of ideas come to you, such as things you need to do, or problems that require solution. If this happens, you may find it helpful to write these things down, releasing your mind and freeing it to focus on listening to God.

Finally, remind yourself that God is with you and start listening to Him within yourself. Focus your attention on Him and listen. What do you hear Him say? I strongly encourage you to read no further until you have taken this step.

Wait in the presence of God and don't be in a rush to leave. Even if you are only listening for a few moments, or a few minutes, it is helpful to adopt a relaxed and unhurried attitude.

Make a mental note of what you hear. The words you receive from God will be the most important words ever spoken to you.

Be open to any impressions you receive as you focus on God. Your experience may involve one or more of the sense modalities, or none of them. It is possible to receive a conviction or certainty about something, a deep inner knowing that a thing is so, and this may or may not be accompanied by inner sight or sound.

Adopt a habit of spending at least five or ten minutes listening to God at the start of each day. Spend longer when you can, and when you are feeling alone, unloved, or upset.

Knowing what you need to know and do

A second fundamental limitation is our finite intelligence. Even the cleverest of us do not have the mindpower to know everything, or if we did, to manipulate all that data within the mind so as to arrive at the most wise and helpful decisions.

On our own we are limited in knowledge, restricted to what we can learn from our own experience and from the communicated experience of others. The sum of human knowledge is finite. Even if we were able to access all the information known to humans (which we cannot), and apply it all (which we cannot), there is no guarantee that we would use it wisely and for the benefit of humankind.

We face two basic problems: the problem of finding out what we really need to know, and the problem of knowing exactly what to do. Not only do we need a way of acquiring salient information, but we need simple, clear, step-by-step directions in applying that knowledge.

Someone may say, "Surely the internet can help us here," but the internet does not, and cannot, fulfil this need. It certainly can provide us with a great deal of information, but it can neither select the exact information we need to know on each occasion, nor tell us exactly how we should apply that information in our particular circumstances. The reason for this is that search engines, like encyclopaedias, are limited in intelligence. A search engine will typically provide you with a large number of results from your search (often in the millions), but you have to choose which results to look at, as well as how to apply whatever information you find.

To solve our two problems we need a source of infinite knowledge that is also immensely intelligent, has a benevolent attitude towards us, and will provide us with the information we really need to know, as well as clear step-by-step guidance in what to do, on a daily basis.

We have already been introduced to this Source, for the same Infinite Intelligence that feeds the spirit, also illuminates and guides the mind.

Make it your discipline to listen to Him daily, and as you listen, He will tell you what you need to know, and guide you in what to do. What you hear will not necessarily be what you *want* to hear, or what you *expect* to hear, but if you are listening to Heaven it will be what you *need* to hear. Those who listen to the Source, and do what He says are the most successful people on earth. The greatest mind is the mind inspired by the Spirit.

The author of a play trusts that the actors will know their lines and follow them. Each will bring to the part their own unique personality, gifts, and skills, but they will not write their own lines, choosing rather to follow the inspiration of the creator. The director of a film trusts that the cast will follow directions, or the message of the film will be blurred and its impact weakened. If we respect the words of earthly authors and the guidance of earthly directors, how much more should we seek and follow the Creator and Director of all things?

Whose production are you in? Your own, God's, or someone else's? If you follow the Director you will play your true role on the stage of life.

But how can you be sure that it is God you are listening to? As you practice listening daily, you will gradually learn to distinguish between the different voices that it is possible to hear in your head. I wish I could say that there were only two voices, your own and God's, but the reality is a little more complex.

There is another spiritual force at work on earth, a dark force that seeks to deceive and destroy. The Devil, or Satan, although limited in knowledge, power, and presence, commands a network of demons committed to your hurt. These dark forces may speak to us, in some cases impersonating the voice of God, sometimes so convincingly that their satanic origin is not immediately apparent.

Some people are so concerned that they might be deceived by demons and tricked into following the dark side that they give up seeking and listening to Him. This is about as intelligent as forsaking all human company because some people are bad or dangerous. The answer is not to shut our ears, but to learn how to discriminate between speakers. As in the development of most skills, we improve with practice. If we will keep listening, practice, and practice alone, will bring us to proficiency, and to a place where we learn to hear God reliably and consistently.

Thankfully, the forces of light are far stronger than the forces of darkness, and will ultimately restrain them completely. Should you become aware that you are being spoken to by enemy spiritual forces, listen to God and reply to them with the words He gives you. The word you receive from God is like a sharp sword that fights for you in the battles of life, overcoming the dark forces that oppose you, whether they are demons or dysfunctions.

Listen each day in the manner already suggested and you will find that God will show you certain things and help you to see what you need to do. It is a good idea to spend a longer time listening when you are facing particular challenges and opportunities that require direction from Heaven.

Overcoming your fear of death

A third fundamental limitation is the inability to ensure our well being beyond the grave, without help from God.

Fear typically arises as a result of uncertainty over something that is important to us. The question of our continued existence after the death of the physical body, is not only important to us, it is of critical significance to our peace of mind. The threat of total annihilation or that of an eternity in hell strikes terror into the heart. Because of such terrible uncertainties, the fear of death is widely repressed, and is likely one of the fears most repressed by humankind.

In order to overcome this fear, we need answers to two questions. Firstly, the question of whether we have continued conscious existence after death, and secondly, the question of how to ensure that our post-death experience will be a positive one.

Don't wait until you die for answers to these questions. Look now on the Eternal, in the manner suggested in this chapter, and you will receive the answers you need.

Don't live in fear any longer. Face your fear by listening daily to the Eternal and trusting in Him. As you do, the assurance of eternal life will slowly come to fill your heart and soul. If you confess your wrongdoing to God and turn from it, He will forgive you, and you will not need to fear punishment ahead.

As you listen and obey, the fact of your eternal existence and your future home in Heaven will be affirmed. It has to be. Focus too much on the temporal, and it is easy to lose sight of your eternal nature, but contemplate the Eternal, and you will feel increasingly at home in eternity.

Finally

Remember what was said at the start about the need to practice these exercises. Now that you have read the book, put its insights to work for you. These principles are like seeds. Leave them on your bookshelf and they will achieve no more than seed that's left in the barn, but plant them in your life and you will reap the fruit they bear.

This is a book to keep going back to. Because it contains practical guidance on increasing your psychological fitness, you can use it as a reference, referring to specific sections as required and practising the steps suggested, until the principles of maximised mindpower are integrated into your thinking and its disciplines become an automatic part of your everyday life.

Don't try to implement all these principles at once. You can read this book in one sitting (if you wish), but you cannot maximise mindpower in one step. Like life, it's a journey. Take it a step at a time, and enjoy the trip.

www.ingramcontent.com/pod-product-compliance
Lightning Source LLC
Chambersburg PA
CBHW070401240426
43661CB00056B/2497